FOCUS ON THE FAMILY®

where women walked

powerful true stories of women's perseverance and God's provision

Jean Blackmer & Laura Greiner

TYNDALE

Tyndale House Publishers, Inc
Wheaton, Illinois

ISBN: 1-58997-165-5

A Focus on the Family Book Published by
Tyndale House Publishers, Wheaton, Illinois 60189

Focus on the Family books are available at special quantity discounts when purchased in bulk by corporations, organizations, churches, or groups. Special imprints, messages, and excerpts can be produced to meet your needs. For more information, contact: Focus on the Family Sales Department, 8605 Explorer Drive, Colorado Springs, CO 80920; or phone (800) 932-9123.

Editor: Lissa Halls Johnson
Cover Design: Kurt Birky and Joy Olson
Cover Photo (or illustration): Mark Waters

Library of Congress Cataloging-in-
Publication Data
Greiner, Laura Ross, 1963-
   Where women walked : powerful true stories of women's perseverance and God's provision / Laura Ross Greiner and Jean Blackmer.
      p. cm.
Focus on the Family.
   ISBN 1-58997-165-5
   1. Christian women—Biography. I. Blackmer, Jean, 1964- II. Title.
BR1713.G75 2004
270.8'2'0922—dc22
                                                                        2003026290

We want to dedicate this book to the women who shared with us their stories and wisdom. We have felt honored by their willingness to honestly share their hearts with us to encourage and inspire those women who read this book.

We also want to give special thanks to our husbands, Bruce and Zane, and our families for their faithful love and support during this project. Finally, we want to thank our girlfriends for their enthusiasm about this book. Like us, they yearn for wisdom from older women and have been our constant cheerleaders.

Contents

Introduction
Where Women Walked

Most young women are eager to experience all life has to offer. They've dreamed about living independently, traveling, attending college, working, falling in love, marrying, having babies, and raising a happy family. Finally, they reach a point where it is time to experience all the exciting opportunities they've dreamed about. So they jump into life headfirst, fearless and confident. After a while they find life is not exactly what they expected. They find it surprises them with ups and downs, joys and disappointments. They also discover that many of the exciting experiences in their life challenge them beyond what they could have imagined.

How does a woman cope with young children whom she loves, but are also demanding? How does a woman encourage a husband who is facing unemployment? How does a woman deal with PMS that threatens to undo her every month? Where can a woman turn for help in the good times and the bad? Where can she go for advice for the big decisions and the daily dilemmas she faces? The questions feel endless. Yet one of the most precious, and overlooked, treasures for her is an older woman who has experienced similar life events—a woman who will offer comfort, guidance, hope, and inspiration because she knows what she's talking about. We believe that learning from women who have walked before us can be invaluable help for navigating through life. And that's why we wrote this book!

Before we began writing, we decided to investigate friendships between older and younger women. We wanted to know "How many young women lack intergenerational friendship in their lives?" We began by hosting an informal focus group of 12 women in their 20s and 30s. After feeding them cherry cobbler, fudge brownies, and strong coffee (nothing gets a woman talking like a good strong cup of coffee), we asked if any of them had an older woman in her life that she could go to for counsel or advice—a mentor. Only one woman out of the 12 had this kind of friend. Next we asked, "If you could sit down with an older woman and ask her one question, what would it be?"

Three hours later our hands ached from furiously taking notes. It was obvious that these young women hungered for information from older women—women who've walked through life before them. They yearned for someone to explain what may lie ahead, to talk openly about life's ups and downs, share their regrets and successes, and give them advice.

After this, we decided to write this book about older women—to write their stories and share the wisdom they gained from their own walks.

The stories we've written are true stories. In some cases we've had to alter details, change names, and employ some fictional techniques like creating dialogue and scenes, but the *essence* of each story has not been changed. Remember, these stories are just tiny snippets of these women's lives; we've barely scratched the surface of wisdom they have to offer.

We started by creating a survey using the questions and issues generated from our original focus group. Because we are Christians, we based the questions for this book and the advice conveyed through its stories on a Christian philosophy of life. In Titus 2:3-5 older women are summoned to teach younger women through relationship and example. Also, in Job 12:12, the Bible emphasizes that aging and experience breed wisdom. "Is not wisdom found among the aged? Does not long life bring understanding?"

We handed out surveys everywhere. We gave them to our friends to give to their mothers and grandmothers. We gave them to older women we knew and respected, and they gave them to their friends. We e-mailed them, distributed them at church groups, and carried them in our cars to give out at any opportunity. As a result, we've met the most fascinating women. We spent countless hours talking to many of them, gathering as much information as we could through phone calls and personal interviews. We shared tears and laughter with so many incredible women. We wish we could tell all their stories, but we can't—like the story of Verlie, who exhibited sheer joy even though she was confined to a bed in a nursing home for the last several years of her life. (She is now in heaven.) Or Roxie, who traveled with her husband and five children around the United States, singing at retirement homes and on radio programs. Or Elbe, who gave birth to her first child while her husband was away fighting in World War II. Nevertheless, we hope that the stories we have included will motivate you to go out and find an older woman to serve as your own guide, friend, and mentor.

We wish to express our gratitude to every woman who filled out our survey and answered our difficult questions. We are humbled by their willingness to be vulnerable and share so openly about their lives and what they have learned.

We hope and pray that you will not only enjoy these stories and quotes, but that they will help you in your own walk through life. Listen to what these women have to say to you, and think about how their walks can impact your own journey. Grab some tissues because some will make you cry, and have a pen handy to answer the thought-provoking questions following each story. But most of all, know that each of these women desires to guide and help you with whatever you're going through. And it is our prayer that you will first be inspired and encouraged by their stories, then motivated to build a relationship with an older woman—your very own guide to help you navigate your walk through life.

chapter one

where women walked . . .

through adversity

Pat

*In the midst of her crisis, Pat made a choice.
She chose to allow God to use her to comfort
others—she chose to become blessed not bitter.*

Pat fought her way through the shroud of sleep to wakefulness. Forcing her eyes open, she heard the sound again. *Who's knocking on the door?*

She groped around in the dark of the unfamiliar hotel room for the light switch next to the bed. "Just a minute!" she called, wondering who would be outside her door at four in the morning. Her heart pounded as she pulled a robe over her sleeveless nightgown, wishing her husband were there with her. *Soon,* she thought. *He'll be here soon.* She padded barefoot across the floor and peered through the peephole before unlatching the door and pulling it open. "What in the world are you two doing here?" she asked her dear friends Curt and Lois. She hugged them both as they entered her little room.

Lois took Pat's hand and led her to the couch. "Pat, sit down. We have something hard to tell you." Pat tried to clear the cobwebs clouding her brain. *Why are they here?*

"Would you like a glass of water?" she asked stifling a yawn. "Or I could get some coffee going."

"No, thanks," Lois said as she sat down and gently tugged Pat down next to her.

Curt sat on her other side and put his arm around her shoulders. "Pat, Ron didn't make it."

"Will he be on the next flight?" Pat asked, assuming they meant he'd missed his flight out of the Philippines.

Her friends remained silent. The dimly lit room inexplicably seemed to grow darker. A wave of nausea swept through her. A cold, clammy hand surrounded her, clenching her in a vise grip.

> *"There comes a point where you have to choose to allow God to make good out of something, or you choose to battle it the rest of your life."—Pat, 58*

"No, Pat, you need to understand," Lois said. "Ron died on the airplane. He's gone to be with the Lord. He isn't coming back."

Through her stunned disbelief, Pat tried to argue. "No, that can't be true. I just talked to him last night before I went to sleep." She looked frantically from Lois to Curt. Confusion swirled through her mind, tangling thoughts together. Fear grew and spread through her until she thought her body would explode.

Ron was coming home from his mission trip. She just knew he was. Sure, he had doubled over from stomach cramps at dinner more than a week ago. But the local doctors had assumed his pain was from a kidney stone. When his pain decreased, they suggested he return home for further treatment. As soon as Pat found out, she did what any wife of 18 years would have done. She began arranging for his every need when he arrived. She chose this hotel because it was close to the airport. It would make picking him up quick and easy. She even arranged for an ambulance and a doctor to be on call in case of an emergency.

Tiny pinpricks tingled up her spine and down her limbs. Lois squeezed her hand. Then Pat realized she had been holding her breath. She wanted desperately for her friends to tell her Ron was okay. That he was on his way home. Instead, they wrapped their arms around her and she began to cry.

"What happened?"

"We're not sure," Curt told her. "We only know that about 30 minutes after the plane left Manila, Ron stood up to get a drink of water. And he collapsed. The director of the mission called us to come tell you and be with you. He didn't want you to be alone. And we didn't want you to go to the airport and hear the news from a stranger."

After a few moments of silence, Lois added, "There was a doctor on board." As if that would ease any pain, erase any questions.

"We'll take you home," Curt said. "As soon as you're ready."

Her friends helped her pack her small overnight bag. They called the front desk and checked her out. As the sun dawned on a new day, Pat felt an eclipse come over her future.

Home was empty. Yet home was full—full of memories. Everywhere she looked, she saw Ron. She opened his closet, and his scent rushed out to meet her. Waking up and seeing his undisturbed pillow made her cry. An anniversary gift he had sent from the Philippines still sat unwrapped on her fireplace mantel with a handwritten note from him that read, "Do not open until I come home." She put off opening it because it meant accepting his death. Finally, she opened the gift and inside the box was a beautiful clock engraved with "Until death do us part." Again, an ocean of tears fell. She wrapped the clock back up, put it back in the box, and placed it in her closet.

Later she learned that as the doctor tried to revive him, Ron drifted in and out of consciousness. Then he grabbed the doctor's arm and weakly whispered his last words, "Don't worry. The Lord's in control." Pat felt comforted by Ron's last words. She believed they were for her from Ron and from the Lord.

Pat moved numbly through the motions of taking care of their four children. Her 15-year-old son became even more absorbed with his friends and activities in hopes of covering up his pain, while her 13-year-old son withdrew to the solitude of his room. Her 11-year-old son cried often, and her eight-year-old daughter thought each time the doorbell rang it might be her dad coming home—she couldn't even begin to comprehend the death of her father at such a young age.

Pat had no answers for their many heart-wrenching questions. Nor could she answer their simple questions like "What's for dinner?"

One night a friend dropped off some baked chicken. Pat stood at the kitchen counter. She couldn't decide if she wanted to make mashed potatoes, scalloped potatoes, or rice to go along with the meal, so she didn't make anything at all.

Her distress over Ron's death only multiplied because it took seven long days for his body to be released from Japan, where the pilots had to make an emergency landing after Ron died on board.

Then, after his body finally arrived, the subsequent autopsy showed Ron didn't have kidney stones. Instead, he had picked up a parasite during his stay in the Philippines that had caused pancreatitis. The disease rapidly moved through his vital organs, destroying them. Because the doctor-prescribed pain medication had improved Ron's symptoms, the physicians recommended he return to the States on a commercial flight rather than a medical plane.

> *"One thing I learned is that everyone grieves differently and the length of the grieving process varies from person to person."*
> —*Pat*

∽

Pat collapsed on her living room couch, sobbing as she clutched the autopsy report to her chest. *God, if You're so good and loving, then why did You make it so clear You wanted Ron to go on this trip and then allow this to happen? Why didn't You answer our prayers for Ron to come home safe?*

These types of questions continually haunted her. The questions grew together to become a thorn-covered wall in her relationship with God. At times anger toward God for allowing Ron to die clouded her thinking. Rage welled up inside her—an emotion she'd never experienced before. She didn't know how to deal with this intense feeling and it scared her.

"This anger you're feeling is a normal part of the grieving process," her counselor told her as Pat sat in the cozy armchair of his office, turmoil roiling through her. "Why don't you go to the flea market and buy a set of breakable dishes? When you feel this anger, break some of them."

The following Saturday Pat wandered around the crowded market, scrounging through boxes of dishes. Out of one cardboard box, she picked up a gaudy glass plate decorated with tacky pink flowers and three big ugly green circles. *These are so ugly I would love to destroy them,* Pat thought as she picked up her unlikely treasure and went to the counter to pay.

A few weeks later Pat was sitting in her backyard at her little umbrella table. Duffy, her cocker spaniel, lay sprawled at her feet while she tried desperately to get something out of reading her Bible. Looking up in frustration, she cried out to God. "Lord, it's been two and a half months since Ron died and I'm not feeling much comfort right now. Please give me some words that will help." Flipping from page to page, she scoured the Bible for encouragement. As comfort eluded her, anger arrived in full force. She flipped to a psalm that infuriated her. Looking up again at the cloudless blue sky and pointing at the opened page, she ranted, "It says here that You are a shelter and fortress, but right now You're not being a shelter and fortress for me! And it says here that You protect those who love You, but You didn't protect Ron!" Anger flooded her spirit like a sudden storm. Her heart began to race.

She marched to the garage and picked up the box of old, gaudy dishes. It took her a moment to decide how far away to stand from her seven-foot wooden fence because she wanted to be close enough to hit it hard, but she didn't want any neighbors to see her. After finding the perfect spot, she put down the old cardboard box, picked up a teacup, and chucked it at the fence. *It does feel good to break something,* she mused as she picked up a plate. Again she faced the fence and said to God, "I hope You're feeling every ounce of my pain right now!" With all the might she could muster from her petite frame, she hurled that plate at the fence. Next, she snatched up another plate and awkwardly threw it like a Frisbee. It smashed against the fence and glass shards rained down to the green grass below. Again and again she hurled the dishes at her target. One time a teacup didn't make it to the fence, so she walked up to where it lay on the ground, grabbed it, and threw it again. With tears streaming down her face she pleaded, "Why did You take Ron away?"

CRASH!

"How do You expect me to get by without him?"

CRASH!

"He was my best friend."

CRASH!

Duffy cocked his head with curiosity and watched her go through this therapeutic outburst. After smashing about a dozen dishes to smithereens, Pat felt tired. She walked over to the fence, knelt down, and began to meticulously pick up all the dish shards. "I don't want the kids to see the mess I've made," Pat said to her pet's ever-listening ears. "It might scare them to know their mom was throwing ugly dishes at a fence." After picking up all the pieces, she collapsed, exhausted, into her chair under the umbrella. She stroked Duffy's soft ear as he laid his head on her lap. She sighed and said, "Well, Duffy, I guess I can spend the rest of my life breaking dishes, or I can decide what God wants to do with the broken pieces of my heart."

Then a realization dawned. Throughout life, people are faced with numerous choices, and now she faced a crucial choice. *How am I going to respond to God with this tragedy? Am I willing to trust God to use even this tragedy in my life and the lives of my children to make us more like Jesus?* As she pondered these questions, she thought about how Jesus and God had to be separated for God's will to be completed. They also did not like that separation. Pat hated what was happening. She didn't want to be separated from Ron, but she also didn't want to live her life as an angry, bitter person. So, she decided to look to God for comfort rather than for the answers to all her "why?" questions at this moment in her life.

She closed her eyes, took a deep breath, and said a prayer of faith, not from her feelings. "God, I choose to let You use me, broken heart and all. To use all of this somehow for good." At that moment she chose to become blessed not bitter.

From then on, Pat began making headway in her ability to function normally again. For quite some time, her friends had brought her meals, but now it was time for her to do her own shopping and cooking. As she pushed her cart through the grocery store, she

> *"I have seen enough bitter people in my life, and I knew I had the choice to become a blessing or to become bitter. I wanted to become a blessing."—Pat*

stopped and placed a package of taco shells on top of her pile of food. She reached for a bottle of picante sauce—Ron's favorite salsa. Pat burst into tears. Feeling weak-kneed she plopped down right in the middle of the aisle. People rushed by, ignoring her heaped in a pile and weeping on the dirty grocery floor. No one stopped to ask if she needed help. She felt completely alone. The fact that no one seemed to care increased her pain.

Finally she stood, brushed the dirt from her black slacks, and was struck with the question *How many people have I walked by in the grocery store who are experiencing intense sorrow?*

This grocery-store-floor realization opened Pat's heart. She began to ask God how she could comfort others. Rather than focusing on her own pain, she determined to become aware of other people's pain—to not ignore those who are hurting.

Today, every time she visits the grocery store, Pat sends up a little prayer for anyone who might need encouragement. She continually prays to have the eyes to see what help others need.

One time while shopping in a department store, she noticed a woman huddled alone in a corner. The woman's eyes were closed and her head rested on her hand. Pat boldly approached her and asked, "Excuse me. I was wondering. Is there anything I can do for you?"

Slightly startled, the woman opened her moist eyes, looked intently at Pat, and said. "Yes, please pray for me." She offered no more information.

"I will pray for you," Pat replied. "I just didn't want you to leave this store not knowing that someone cares about you."

Through the years Pat slowly adjusted to life without her beloved. But the pain never totally disappeared. Even during times of celebration—like when her daughter won a swim race, her oldest son married, or when her other sons hit their first home runs—she longed to share those moments with Ron.

> *"In Isaiah 43:2, it reads 'when' you pass through the waters, I will be with you, and 'when' you walk through the fire, you will not be burned. It doesn't say 'if.' So, trust in God—not to prevent anything bad, but to walk with you through everything."—Pat*

⌒

Thirteen years after Ron's death, Pat's eyes still well up with tears at the memories and reminders of him. She still wears her wedding ring. The clock he sent her from the Philippines still sits in a dark closet. It's too vivid a reminder that Ron's death tore them apart earlier than she ever would have imagined. The pain is different now but will always be there because of the great love they shared. Yet Pat faithfully clings to her choice to allow God to use her tragedy to help others.

Today, Pat counsels women in crisis and speaks to women's groups all over the world. She is quick to laugh and quick to cry, depending on what the moment or person in need requires. "It is through this time in my life that I learned to pray my most honest, authentic, heartfelt prayers to God. Not all the stuff in our lives is 'caused' by God, but all things are filtered by Him. What happens to us outwardly is not nearly as important as what happens to us inwardly. God goes through all our pains with us and then graciously uses them to make us more like Him." Because of these lessons, Pat embraces each opportunity the Lord gives her to help those with painful loss—those just like her.

"Don't ask the person grieving how you can help; they won't be able to tell you. Instead ask God to give you wisdom and insight for ways of helping."—Pat

In Their Footsteps

"My youngest son was hit by a car when he was six years old. We were told that if he lived, it was possible that he would not be educable. After we were dismissed from the hospital, I spent the whole night painting a picture of 'the lilies of the field.' 'They toil not, neither do they spin . . .' I spent the night claiming the promises of Matthew 6. Painting kept my mind and hands busy and diffused the dragons of worry and replaced them with faith."

—Anonymous, 66

"Try not to look inward at all the pain and suffering and hurt you are going through, but look to the Lord for strength to make it through the next moment."

—Stephanie, 59, who has experienced emotional pain
from her relationship with her mother

"It seems to me that when times were difficult and I was willing to go to the Lord and surrender to Him, He taught me great things about Himself. Very often ministry comes out of our deepest trials. Elisabeth Elliot has said, 'Learn to accept things the way you don't want them to be.'"

—Jackie, 63

"Unfortunately, trials seem to be the tool God uses often to lead us closer to Him and to deepen our faith. It is always our choice: We can accept with open heart and hands what God brings, which will result in joy, or we can try and ignore or reject His lessons, which will result in bitterness."

—Donna, 54, who ministers to women in a large
church in North Carolina

Betty

*Through the tragic loss of her daughter, Betty learned to
stop asking the difficult question "Why, God?"*

"Betty," a soft voice whispered. Startled, Betty opened her eyes.

"Yes?" she answered, wondering why the church receptionist would
interrupt her in the middle of praying with her Bible study leadership
group.

"There is an urgent call for you from your husband."

Getting up from her knees, she hurried to the church telephone.
"Don?"

"Betty, I just got a call from a doctor in Aberdeen. He said Cyndy
is in the hospital and in a coma." He paused, his voice choked with
emotion. "He said she is gravely ill. I told him we'd come at once."

Her thoughts and her heart raced all at once. "I'm coming home
right now," she said, hanging up the phone. She needed to get home.
She needed to get to Cyndy, her 23-year-old daughter who was in Scot-
land visiting friends during her graduate school semester break.

After a Bible study friend drove her home, Betty immediately
began packing her suitcase while Don filled her in on what little he had
learned from the neurosurgeon. "She had a brain hemorrhage this

morning." Pausing, his eyes brimmed with tears. "He said she might be gone before we can arrive from California."

Lord, please keep Cyndy alive until we reach her, Betty prayed in desperation as she frantically threw things into her suitcase.

On the plane Betty and Don clutched each other's hands and cried silently together. Tears streaming down her face, Betty again pled with the Lord to let Cyndy live. *Why, Lord? Why would You allow her to die when she is so devoted to You and doing Your ministry work?* Betty had often marveled at her daughter's spiritual maturity at such a young age. It seemed Cyndy was always leading a Bible study or doing ministry work. She couldn't imagine why God would take someone who loved to serve Him so much.

As pain and anguish gripped her, Betty clung to the truths she knew about God. *Lord, I know You love Cyndy even more than I do, and I lift her up to You for Your perfect will to be done in her life. Please give me the grace to accept Your will if it is different from mine.* When Betty uttered this prayer, a powerful peace—even joy—swept over her as the plane hummed over the Atlantic Ocean. *That's You, Lord. I could only feel this way through You,* she murmured through her tears with a faint smile.

When the plane finally landed in Aberdeen, the family Cyndy had been visiting greeted Betty and Don. "Cyndy's alive!" said Gillian, the mother of Cyndy's friend. Betty let out a shuddering breath as Gillian continued. "She is still in a coma but somewhat stabilized." Gillian's warm embrace and encouraging words gave Betty hope.

As they drove to the hospital, Betty tried to prepare herself for what it would be like to see Cyndy, her vivacious daughter, in the intensive care unit in a coma. When she walked into the room, her heart broke. Her daughter lay motionless with her beautiful ash blonde hair spread across the pillow. Tubes and machines and bottles surrounded her. Feeling weak, Betty sunk into a chair, put her head down on Cyndy's bed, and wept. *She's such a devoted servant. Why, Lord? Why?* Her broken sobs were muffled by the bed.

With her head still buried in the bed, Betty felt a hand gently resting on her shoulder. Looking up, she saw the compassionate face of the head nurse. "Talk to Cyndy," she said in her rich Scottish brogue. "Stroke her arm. Hold her hand. She will hear your voice and feel your touch."

Wiping her tears with a tissue, Betty sat up and took her daughter's hands in her own. "Honey, we're here. Dad and I are right here with you. We love you, Cyndy. We're going to take care of you." Standing up, she bent over and kissed Cyndy's forehead then wiped her own tears from Cyndy's face.

The next day the neurosurgeon told Betty and Don that he would not know what caused the brain hemorrhage without doing extensive brain surgery. They all agreed it wasn't a good idea. Their first priority was to get Cyndy stabilized and fly her home. But a persistent fever kept Cyndy in the Aberdeen hospital for two and a half months.

> *"I felt confident that if any word would get through the darkness of Cyndy's coma, God's Word would."—Betty, 67*

As the days passed, Betty fell into a daily routine with Cyndy. She arrived at the hospital early in the morning to bathe her. Then she spent an hour or two each morning reading her Scripture, praying with her, and listening to praise music. One morning, as she pulled a chair up to the hospital bed, Betty said, "Cyndy, I was reading from Isaiah last night. Listen to this verse." Opening her Bible, she read Isaiah 26:3: "You will keep in perfect peace him whose mind is steadfast, because he trusts in you." Her eyes glistened as she read the words again. Looking up from the book to her comatose daughter, Betty felt what God promised. In the midst of such sorrow, a blanket of comfort was wrapped around her heart. "Cyndy, we need to keep our eyes on Him. If we keep glued to Him, He will give us peace."

Cyndy began to show signs of improvement in her coma. Finally, her fever subsided and she was given clearance to be transported to

California. As Betty rode on the plane with Cyndy, she again clung to the truths of God's Word and the hope that once back in the United States, Cyndy would continue to recover.

New doctors took over Cyndy's care in a San Diego hospital. After a battery of new tests and a brain biopsy, Cyndy's neurosurgeon asked Betty and Don to meet him in the hospital lobby. Sitting in the corner of the lobby, the doctor spoke softly. "I am sorry to have to tell you this but we have found a tumor in Cyndy's brain. That is what caused her hemorrhage. You need to know that it is malignant and inoperable. We have no way to treat it." With kind eyes the doctor spoke with compassion. "Take her home now. Make her as comfortable as possible. It shouldn't be long."

Although Betty was not completely surprised, the reality of his words slapped her so hard she couldn't move or talk for a long moment. She sat motionless as people walked by her carrying on with life. *Why, Lord? She loves You and has such a ministry here on earth.*

Several minutes after the doctor had walked away, Betty mechanically made her way toward the pay phones. She needed to make some calls to tell their family and friends what the doctor had said. Collapsing onto the hard plastic chair in the phone booth, she closed her eyes. After sitting alone in the booth for several minutes, she felt God give her a clear message. *Don't deny that I am going to take Cyndy. Accept it, Betty, and I will hold your hand and walk you through the time ahead. If you are in denial, you will miss My guidance and all that I have to teach you.*

> *"Acceptance brings peace."—Betty*
>
> ∽

Betty sat for a long time soaking in this message. She had seen people in denial over death before. *It only prolongs the suffering, Lord, doesn't it?*

The following week as Betty and Don were preparing to bring Cyndy home, Betty got into her car to drive to the hospital and fill out some paperwork. As she slid into the driver's seat, all of a sudden Betty had a compulsion to open up her Bible and read from Isaiah 55. She needed to get to the hospital, but the compulsion was too strong to ignore. She reached to the passenger seat, picked up her Bible, and flipped the pages until she reached Isaiah. When her eyes fell on verse 8, she began to pull the words inside her, letting them speak to her heart.

"For my thoughts are not your thoughts, neither are your ways my ways," declares the LORD. "As the heavens are higher than the earth, so are my ways higher than your ways and my thoughts than your thoughts. As the rain and the snow come down from heaven, and do not return to it without watering the earth and making it bud and flourish, so that it yields seed for the sower and bread for the eater, so is my word that goes out from my mouth: It will not return to me empty, but will accomplish what I desire and achieve the purpose for which I sent it." (8-11)

Tears welled up in her eyes and the words sank in. *I will never understand Your ways, Lord. That is not my job. My job is to trust You. That's all.* As the tears spilled down her cheeks, she felt God speaking directly to her heart. At that moment she ceased questioning why God would take Cyndy, who loved Him so much. She would never understand, but she would trust. Taking a deep breath, Betty closed her eyes and prayed. *If I keep asking "why?" I won't really be able to accept Cyndy's death, will I, Lord? And it will keep me distracted from You.* Betty smiled through her tears as His peace once again encircled her.

That afternoon they transported Cyndy home in an ambulance. Riding with her, Betty recited the words of Isaiah over again in her mind. As she looked down at her sleeping daughter's still face, her heart agonized. She didn't know how long she would have her, but she took God at His word and clung to His ways, His purposes, not hers. *Lord, I hate this. I wish it were me dying and not my beautiful Cyndy. But I trust You,* she whispered softly as she stroked her daughter's cheek.

Contrary to the doctor's prediction, Cyndy lived six more agonizing months. On a quiet February afternoon she lay peacefully in her bed at home as her family sat holding her hands. Praise music softly played in the background. As Cyndy took her final breath, the lyrics ministered to Betty: "We are standing on holy ground, and I know there are angels all around." Even though Betty felt grateful Cyndy's struggle was over, her heart splintered into little broken pieces.

After Cyndy's memorial service Betty looked to her church for a grief support ministry but found none. Without a group to turn to Betty decided she would rely on God alone to direct and guide her through her immense heartache and grief. This turned out to be an incredible journey, which led Betty to develop this story into her own book, *God's Grip in Grief* (copyrighted, 1997). She now also coordinates a grief ministry in her own church as well as trains grief group leaders and assists other churches with starting grief ministries.

> *"Trust comes from knowing someone, and I knew my Father. I knew His character is trustworthy."—Betty*

Today Betty is still in awe of how God is using her journey through Cyndy's illness and death to minister to people. "As I entered that frightening territory that all parents dread, I clung to God's guidebook (the Bible) to get me through. And slowly but steadily, He gave me a road map filled with more than 200 verses on how to walk through my journey of loss. It is such a blessing to share that with others through my book and ministry."

In Their Footsteps

"We expect fairness in this life, but we live in a fallen world that is full of injustices. But God can turn anything around and use it."
—*Edie, 67*

"God can work through times of loss. There is a beauty to being able to look back on a time of loss and see that God was working. You don't know it at the time, but later you can often see the good."
—*Sharon, 65*

"I have gone through so much in my life, but I can still say life is wonderful because I have God. I see Him in people all around me."
—*Susan, 44, whose three-year-old son drowned*

"You can use any tragedy in life as a stumbling block or a stepping stone."
—*Ruby, 68*

Jane

*Jane suffers from multiple sclerosis (MS). Over a period of
28 years, the disease has robbed her of control over her
body. The resulting loss of so many things in this life has
given Jane a new appreciation for the hope of eternal life.*

Jane laced up her well-worn tennis shoes. She glanced at her watch. She
needed to hurry to be on time for her early morning walk with her
neighbor Linda. She stepped outside, pausing to take a deep breath,
inhaling the scent of spring. It always felt good to be out in the fresh
air. The steroids the doctor had prescribed to help her newly diagnosed
multiple sclerosis (MS) felt like a miracle drug. Her right leg no longer
dragged and the muscles in both her legs felt strong. She hummed a
praise hymn as she hustled over to meet Linda.

After a two-mile, hilly speed walk, Jane felt invigorated. She show-
ered and then hopped into her car, racing over to the church for organ
practice. When Mel, her husband, came home that evening, she had
the house meticulously cleaned and a piping hot meal waiting for him
on the table.

That night when she tried to fall asleep, she tossed and turned. The
doctor had told her that a side effect of the steroids could be insomnia.

After several hours of flopping around, she resigned herself to getting up and doing something. She climbed out of bed and padded into the kitchen. After pouring herself a glass of water, she headed into the living room and curled up on her favorite oversized chair. Picking up her journal she began to write.

A few days ago I was diagnosed with MS. Instead of feeling devastated, I feel relieved. Now I have an answer to all the weird things my body has been doing. I don't feel frightened about the future either because the doctor says MS is different for everyone. He looked at my chart and said that ten years ago, they thought I might have MS but weren't 100 percent sure. I've been fine this long so I'm not worried. Right now I feel better than ever.

Jane continued to feel great for several months until she relapsed. Her left leg began to drag again but this time it seemed worse. The doctors prescribed steroids once more and her gait returned to normal within two days. Yet when the steroid treatment ended, she needed a cane to support her wobbly stride.

The pattern of relapsing, obtaining steroids, then returning to nearly normal went on for many years. The heavy doses of steroids reduced the inflammation and served as an effective short-term solution, allowing Jane to live a normal life. She still played the organ, walked every morning, and ran an orderly house. Gradually though, as her legs grew weaker, she started scaling back her walks to a flat half-mile loop. In time, even this became too difficult.

One morning before she started out on the dirt trail, her legs felt more tired than usual. She dismissed the fatigue and forged ahead, refusing to give in to her weakening muscles.

Halfway through her walk she panicked. Her legs had grown so tired that she didn't think she could take one more step. She stopped walking and closed her eyes, concentrating on her body. She hadn't imagined it. Her legs felt like they might buckle. *I'm not going to be able to get back to my car,* she thought. Frantic, she looked around for something to hold on to. She saw an outhouse 100 yards away. *Come on,*

Jane. You can make it there. Step by slow, agonizing step, she moved toward it. She grabbed on to the building with both arms. She inched herself around it until she came to the other side.

She looked around for the next thing she could cling to. She saw a post several yards up the path. *Jane, you can make it to the post,* she coaxed herself. Limping to the post, she felt her legs were like rubber bands. *I'm going to have to crawl back to the car,* she thought with dread. But she made it to the post and hung on for dear life. After resting for several minutes she staggered over the remaining distance to her car. Opening the car door she collapsed onto the driver's seat. *I can't do this anymore,* she thought, leaning her head against the steering wheel.

> *"I identify with David in the Psalms when he pours his heart out to God. He is honest with God about his struggles. That is a comfort to me because there are definite seasons where I have really struggled."*—Jane, 52

↝

The next morning when Jane couldn't take a walk of any length, a dark cloud settled over her. She felt sick at heart. *What else am I going to lose?* she wondered, staring out the family room window at the crisp autumn day. She shoved the thought away and walked out onto the back deck. Fresh air would make her feel better. Looking out at the pine trees, she tried to keep her thoughts positive. But she couldn't shake the deep loss that burrowed inside her. Walking had made her feel healthy and normal.

Jane's mind swirled around questions about her future. Her life felt out of her control. *It's getting so much worse,* she thought, as a bubble of panic popped inside her. *What's next?* She clung to self-control and forced the thoughts of a bleak future from her mind. But even after the thoughts were banned, her body still trembled. Clinging to one of her favorite Bible verses, she whispered, *Be still, and know that I am God* (Psalm 46:10). She closed her eyes and concentrated on the words. *Be still, Jane . . . still.*

Jane began using forearm crutches to get around and a scooter to help her navigate around big department stores and the grocery store. At first, the new bulky equipment frustrated her. The forearm crutches felt ugly and embarrassing. Jane found it hard to maneuver the scooter around tight corners and often careened into stores' holiday displays. But as the MS progressed, she grew to appreciate the equipment because she knew that without it, she wouldn't be able to get around by herself at all. It had become her lifeline to the little independence she had left.

Often Jane would call on Linda and her family to help her load the scooter into her van. Jane always felt so grateful for the assistance but at the same time, it was so humbling to need so much aid in everything she did. One afternoon as she watched Linda's healthy body unload her scooter, Jane found it hard not to think about all she once had and now, all she had lost. After she thanked Linda for her help, Jane sat for a long moment watching Linda walk home. Her stride was strong and steady. Looking down at her deteriorating legs she caught herself. *No, Jane,* she told herself. *Don't go down that road.* She made herself hold fast to the verses in 2 Corinthians 4:16-18:

> Therefore we do not lose heart. Though outwardly we are wasting away, yet inwardly we are being renewed day by day. For our light and momentary troubles are achieving for us an eternal glory that far outweighs them all. So we fix our eyes not on what is seen, but on what is unseen. For what is seen is temporary, but what is unseen is eternal.

Yes, Lord, Jane prayed as she wheeled herself inside the house. *These useless legs are only temporary. Help me hold on to all that You have for me that is unseen. Please renew me day by day, Lord. Make me like You.*

Over time the steroids lost their effectiveness. Jane's abilities diminished and her life became more confined to the walls of her home. In front of others she put up a brave front and tried not to let herself dwell on her circumstances. She didn't want to burden Mel, her beloved optimist, with the despondency she felt deep in her soul. Only when she sat alone in the quietness of her house did she allow broken sobs to escape, admitting her deepest fears and frustrations to God.

In time, Jane became so weak that she couldn't walk with any of her disability devices. The forearm crutches went into the closet. Her upper body also weakened so she couldn't lift herself into or out of the scooter, and her hands could no longer operate the controls. Her hands became too weak to play the organ at all and then too stiff to write or use the computer. Totally dependent, Jane battled depression. "From the time I was a little girl I have always just wanted to do it myself," she wept to her counselor. "Now I can't do anything myself."

Jane disliked relying on others to do the tasks in her home that she longed to do. Kind, caring church friends came to clean her house. But when they left, Jane only felt irritated. *They did it all wrong. Nothing is in the right place.* She cringed. They'd mismatched her dishes and stacked them incorrectly. There was nothing she could do about it. MS held her prisoner. Hanging her head down, tears of frustration burned in her eyes as her arms hung uselessly at her sides.

When Mel and Jane ordered a leather-cushioned, state-of-the-art wheelchair, Jane laughed at the seat belt. *Why would I ever need a seat belt?* She couldn't imagine. But as the MS continued to wreak havoc through her body, eventually she was no longer able to hold up her torso by herself. She then found the security of the seat belt welcoming.

Jane now spends her days with a full-time caregiver. Many hours a day are spent on the simple tasks of life like bathing, dressing, and eating. Because Mel works from their home and has several employees coming and going all the time, she is never lonely. Her house is always filled with people. The people in her home help Jane not feel isolated in her confinement. She also has two friends who come to her house and visit with her every week. With both friends she spends time talking about life, sharing struggles, and praying. These visits are a breath of fresh air for Jane and an important source of spiritual nourishment for her.

Throughout her journey of loss Jane has clung to her deep faith. Although she sits stiffly in her wheelchair with little control over her body, her face radiates hope. Her big blue eyes shimmer as she explains, "When I'm feeling helpless I try to remember that we are not going to be here long. This life that we live is fleeting in the grand scheme of things. We have an eternal life awaiting us." Glancing down at her weak arms and legs, she continues with a genuine smile, "This shell will be something we get rid of. We're going to get a new body that is no longer trapped by all the things on us that don't work." She glances at her rigid, unbending hands and says with a voice of confidence, "One day this body will be free again."

Every morning as she waits for her caregiver to arrive, she reminds herself, "Everything in this world is temporal—only Christ is eternal."

Jane's words are an important reminder for any woman traversing through a dark valley in life. This isn't all there is. There is eternal *life* through Jesus Christ.

In Their Footsteps

"I have so much to be thankful for, so that is what I think about. I don't have time to think about anything else."
—*Verlie, 85, who has been confined to a bed in a nursing home for several years*

"Claiming and reciting Scripture helped me through my long illness. Some days I was too sick to get out of my nightclothes. I would just lie on the couch all day. On good days I would go outside and sit in the fresh air. I couldn't read the Bible much during this time, so the Scripture I knew in my heart and my head was all that I had and it helped. It is important to store up Scripture in your heart for this exact reason."
—*Edith, 65*

"I learned not to ask the 'why me?' questions (in this imperfect world 'why not me?' is a more valid question). And God was very faithful in giving me guidance, direction, and answers to my 'now what?' and 'how do I deal with this?' questions."
—*Dora, 50, whose life was threatened by breast cancer*

"When I was a child I thought heaven sounded so boring, but I preferred heaven to hell. I now know that my excessive God is so extreme that He will have prepared for me sights and sounds that even I cannot imagine. He is the master of special effects. Big will be bigger, sound will be amplified, glitter will be glitter-ier, and color will sweep a canvas too big for me to comprehend."
—*Anonymous*

Lorraine B.

When Lorraine's son-in-law, Todd Beamer,
died in the terrorist attacks on 9/11, Lorraine knew
from the sudden death of her own husband
what the future held for her daughter Lisa.

Driving through the drenching rain, Lorraine gripped the steering wheel of her car as her two grandchildren slept peacefully in the backseat. *I'm so glad the boys are sleeping. I guess I did a good job of wearing them out.* The wipers swished back and forth across the windshield, providing brief moments of clarity in the downpour. Lorraine leaned forward, trying to capture those moments to see the yellow and white road lines. *I'll sure be relieved when I see Todd. I hate driving this road— especially in the rain.*

For the past five days Lorraine had cared for Lisa and Todd's two boys while her daughter and son-in-law vacationed in Italy. Tonight, September 10, she was returning the worn-out toddlers to their parents. Within the past month Lorraine had sent her fourth child, Jonathan, off to college. She couldn't believe it. Tonight, after dropping off her grandchildren, she would officially be an empty-nester.

September 11th is going to be the first day of the rest of my life! she thought. *Without anymore children at home, I'll be able to do the things I've put off for years. I can spend more time building my counseling ministry. I'll have more time with my friends. But it will be a little strange to live alone.*

Alone. Alone after her children left home was not what she would have imagined for her life. But more than 18 years before, Lorraine's husband, Paul, had died suddenly, leaving her to raise their four children, ages two to 15 years. After his death, she'd poured her life into her children. She went back to school to get her master's degree in counseling and worked hard to provide for them. Now, all of her children were grown and gone out of the house. This night marked the end of a chapter in her life. And tomorrow marked the beginning of a new era.

> *"Every situation is an opportunity for you. Even if it doesn't feel like it at the moment, it's an opportunity to get to know God better, to become the person God intends you to be, and to comfort someone else with the comfort you have received from God."—Lorraine, 58*

◑◐

After a 45-minute drive she turned her car into the designated meeting spot and pulled into the parking space next to Todd and Lisa's van. Todd smiled and waved to her. *Thank You, Lord, we made it,* she thought as she took a deep breath of relief. Todd jumped out of the car and dashed through the pouring rain to transfer the kids from her car to his. Lorraine got out to help, and within a few moments, she was soaking wet.

Neither wanted to stand out in the pouring rain and chat, but Lorraine was anxious to ask at least one question: "Did you have fun on your trip?"

"Yes!" answered Todd. That was the last word she ever heard him utter.

She watched Todd's back as he climbed in the side door of the mini-van and buckled the two boys into their car seats. "I'll call Lisa when I get home and get the details," Lorraine said as she dashed back to the warmth and shelter of her car.

When she returned home, she called Lisa.

"Thanks, Mom. It was wonderful to spend time alone with Todd. We had a great time. Tomorrow he's back to work. He has to fly to California."

"No, don't let him go. You just got back," Lorraine said.

"I know, but he has to go. He was supposed to go tonight but he wanted to see the boys, so he's flying out tomorrow and then back tomorrow night."

"Wow, I don't know how he does it. Well, I'll call you tomorrow. I love you."

The next morning Lorraine woke up to a bright sunny day. *What an absolutely gorgeous day,* Lorraine thought as she drove to work. *Glad the rain finally stopped.* She switched on her car radio to catch some news. The big story of the morning was the comeback of Michael Jordan— Todd's favorite basketball player. *I bet Todd's excited about this news. But if that's all they're talking about, it must be a really slow news day*, she concluded.

After meeting with her first client, Lorraine sat down at her desk to catch up on some paperwork. Dave, the assistant pastor, came into her office and announced, "Did you hear that a plane crashed into the World Trade Center?"

"No, I've been with a client. Was it some kind of accident?" she asked.

"I'm not sure. I'm going to go back to my office to listen to the news."

A few moments later, he again appeared in the doorway of her office, offering news bites as he heard them. "The other tower just got hit. They think it's terrorists. They're saying the planes were hijacked and then flown into the towers." He disappeared for a moment and then popped his head back into her office. "Lorraine, this is unbelievable! I'm following the news updates on my computer if you want to come and see."

Lorraine stared at her pile of papers, trying to comprehend what he had just said. Then Bev, Pastor Dennis's wife, came into her office to give her more of the unbelievable news.

"I just heard another plane hit the Pentagon, and another plane crashed in a field in Pennsylvania." Bev's voice choked with emotion. "They're shutting down all the airports. No planes are being allowed to take off."

A sudden fear gripped Lorraine's heart. *Oh no. Todd was flying today. I need to go call Lisa.* Lorraine's heart began pounding in her chest like a drum. She had a very bad feeling as she dialed Lisa's number. *Busy. Not a good sign. Lord, please let Todd be okay.* A few moments after hanging up, her phone rang. It was Lisa. "Oh, Mom, I think Todd was on the plane that crashed in Pennsylvania."

"No! That can't be." Lorraine couldn't believe it. She wouldn't believe it until she knew for certain.

"Yes," Lisa managed to say.

"I'm coming down to be with you," Lorraine said as she paced around the room, trying to remain calm.

"No, Mom, you're not going to be able to get here; all the roads are closed."

"Somehow I will get there. I'm coming."

"No, Mom, please. I can't let something happen to you, too," Lisa sobbed.

"Honey, don't worry about me. I'll be okay. I'll go by home and pick up a few things then come down to your house."

Just a couple of minutes after Lorraine arrived home, Bev and Dennis drove up and insisted on driving her to Lisa's home. A drive that normally took two hours now took four. The major highways were closed so they had to travel through little towns and make their way from Lorraine's home in New York to Lisa's in New Jersey. During the entire drive, Lorraine sat in silence. She felt numb. She didn't *want* to feel anything. It was just too painful. The pain felt so familiar—one she never wanted to feel again—the pain she had felt when Paul died.

Lorraine remembered it too well. It was a normal start to a beautiful day, just like today. In the usual morning rush of a household with four small children, Lorraine gave Paul a kiss on his cheek as he left for work. About an hour later she received a call that he had collapsed and had been rushed to the hospital. She hurried to be with him. When she arrived, Paul was awake and talking. The doctor in the emergency room didn't seem too concerned, but he wanted to keep Paul overnight just for observation. Lorraine had to get back and take care of the kids. So she left him in the doctor's care.

The next morning at 5:30 the doctor called and said, "Paul took a turn for the worse last night. Things are very bad. We're moving him to another hospital with better facilities to treat him."

"I'll be right there," Lorraine said.

"It would probably be better if you didn't leave your house right now. Just in case we need to reach you."

Lorraine woke her four children. Lisa, 15 years old; Paul, 14; Holly, 10; and Jonathan, almost two. They gathered in Lisa's room and prayed for Paul. Just as Lorraine said, "Amen," the phone rang. It was the doctor.

"Lorraine, I'm sorry to have to tell you this. We didn't have a chance to move Paul. He died." Lorraine felt a wave of shock spread through her body. Then she went numb. Tears didn't fall. She didn't want to cry in front of her kids. *If I sit down and cry right now, I'll never stop crying,* she thought. Instead, before returning to the hospital, she quickly vacuumed her living room carpet. She knew lots of people would be coming over and she wanted her house to be clean.

Now here she was driving to be with her daughter and grandchildren whose husband and father had suddenly been taken away. To make matters worse, Todd's life, and the lives of so many other innocent people, were cut short by a suicidal act of terrorists. It all seemed so evil and unjust. *How can people do this to other human beings?* she wondered. Disbelief of what was happening filled her mind. *Don't let this be true. No, this is not happening,* she thought to herself over and over again. She stared out the window and saw military vehicles and soldiers all over the place. It *was* happening.

Already, Lisa's house was filled with people. Cars lined the street. Food and flowers filled the kitchen.

"Where's Lisa?" Lorraine asked Lisa's friend.

"She's upstairs in her room. She wanted to be alone."

Lorraine climbed the stairs to Lisa's closed door. She gently knocked and then slowly opened up the door to the bedroom. Lisa was sitting on her bed, staring out the window. Lost. Alone. Confused. And five months pregnant.

> *"I didn't give the terrorists much thought at all. Because they had already hurt my family to the core, I didn't want to allow them to hurt us any more. I didn't want to give them any of my time or energy."*—Lorraine

⁐

Lisa couldn't even speak. Lorraine went over to her, enfolded Lisa in her arms, and said, "Whatever you need from me I will give to you." They sat on the bed together in somber silence. No words could convey the deep, painful emotions they both felt. Lorraine kept thinking, *I feel like I'm looking at myself 18 years ago. I have gone through this. I know what lies ahead for her. I know she doesn't even know what she needs, but I do. I will take care of her and her babies. Whatever they need, I will do it.*

Lorraine sat on Lisa's bed, holding back her own tears and holding Lisa. Lots of people filled Lisa's house but none knew Lisa like Lorraine knew Lisa. Now, it was time to use her past experience of losing her husband to comfort her own daughter.

For the next three weeks, Lorraine stayed with Lisa and the children. She spent most of the days taking care of her two grandsons. People came and went in droves. After finding out the sketchy details of Todd's last heroic moments on the airplane, the media frenzy began. Lorraine watched in amazement as her daughter became a spokesperson and symbol of hope to America after the tragic terrorist attack.

One time Lorraine commented to Lisa, "God really has a special thing for you and Todd to do."

"But why?" Lisa asked.

"I don't know why. But look at you. You're doing it!"

Phone calls, letters, packages came nonstop. People sent packages from all over the world. Sometimes they were addressed simply to "Wife of Hero Todd Beamer, USA." Lorraine tried to help Lisa keep up with the incoming support, but that became too much. They gave up trying to respond to all of the phone calls and letters. Requests poured in for Lisa to speak or do interviews on television. It became so hectic that Lorraine practically had to make an appointment to speak with Lisa. But she felt proud of Lisa's strength and composure as she spoke to various groups.

One of Lorraine's main concerns was that Lisa wouldn't be able to properly mourn for Todd. When Paul died, Lorraine felt she never took the time to completely mourn his death. She was thrust into taking care of her kids. She tried to be strong but in this attempt, she regrets she never allowed herself to mourn. She watched as Lisa was thrust into the public eye and felt a twinge of apprehension for her.

> *"Evil is prevalent, but God is in control and He is going to deal with evil at some point."*
> *—Lorraine*

ᕲᕔ

One morning, just a little more than a week after 9/11, Lisa and Lorraine sat side by side on a bus taking them and other family members of those who died in the attack to the crash site in Pennsylvania.

"Mom, you know a lot of media opportunities are coming my way. I'm going to appear on another news program tonight," Lisa explained.

Lorraine felt again a little twinge of apprehension. *Lord, I never could have done what Lisa is doing after Paul died. But I'm not Lisa. I have to entrust her to You. I know You will use her and Todd through this, no matter how painful it is. She has to make her own decisions. Help me help her to follow You.* After this quiet moment of trying to let go of her control of Lisa and her desire to protect her from the pain she faced, Lorraine asked Lisa one question: "Lisa, why are you doing all of this? What do you see as your purpose?"

Lisa knew exactly why and what she desired—what motivated her to accept the attention and speak out as much as possible. "I want to create a legacy for my children, for them to know and remember their dad was a hero. And I want to use this opportunity to tell people about our faith in the Lord. I know that's what Todd would want me to do."

"Lisa, those are all good reasons. I'll take the boys or do whatever you need me to do," Lorraine answered. "I'm here for you. And I'm here for the boys. I love being with them. Even after all this attention dies down, I'll be here for you as long as you need me."

For the next 18 months, Lorraine worked Monday through Thursday and usually spent Thursday evening until Sunday evening with Lisa, her two boys, and her little girl, born four months after Todd died.

The key thought in her mind when she lost Paul, which resurfaced when Todd died, was "Don't waste this. Even though I hate this and I never would have chosen this—I don't want to waste it. I want to get out of it whatever God wants me to."

Like mother, like daughter. Lisa has used Todd's death as an opportunity to tell others about her faith in God. And Lorraine has used it as a time to minister to her daughter and grandchildren. She treasures the amount of time she gets to spend with them—the opportunity to get to know them and have an impact on their lives.

One morning, following a meeting with a public relations specialist, Lisa sat down at her kitchen table and told Lorraine, "Mom, there are still lots of media opportunities for me to speak, but I feel like I've pretty much said everything I have to say. I've decided not to do as much as before. I want to devote myself to my children."

"Lisa, in everything I've seen you do—get up and speak without even preparing and saying the perfect thing—you are amazing. When your dad died, I could never have gotten up and talked about it the way you have about Todd. I've been amazed and inspired by your strength. God is definitely using you in incredible ways. Who knows what God will still do with you?"

Lorraine certainly understood Lisa's desire to put her family first. That's what Lorraine did when her own husband died. But again, Lorraine didn't feel she could give Lisa advice. She listened, praised her for her gifts, and encouraged her to find her own path through her grief.

Lorraine has found her new life—not the one she expected right now, but one of deep fulfillment, of continuing to look at every circumstance as an opportunity to grow. She never imagined she would have to watch her own daughter deal with the death of her husband during such a tragic time in American history, but from her own experience, she provides the comfort of a wise counselor and of a loving, wise mom.

> *"The process of mourning is a long process, but God is with us in our mourning. He mourns with us. I knew God before, but now I know Him at a different level."*—Lorraine

In Their Footsteps

"My daughter was molested at a young age, and so was I. It has strangely been a wonderfully bonding experience. I am able to give her wisdom when she doesn't understand her actions/reactions. I can also give her hope that she will survive the horrendous pain that comes with walking through the memories and finding healing. I'm not glad I went through that situation myself, but being able to help my daughter has given the experience value."
—*Cathy, 50*

"Through many challenging life experiences, I have had to rely on the Lord to sustain me. The head knowledge of His mighty power has grown to heart knowledge."
—*Anonymous*

"Always have room in your life for the Lord. As circumstances change, He is always there for you."
—*Anonymous, 63*

Adversity Summary

⌒

Life is hard. Jesus didn't say, "In this world you *might* have trouble." He said, "In this world you *will* have trouble. But take heart! I have overcome the world" (John 16:33, emphasis added). The older a woman is, the greater the possibility that she has suffered through some sort of major adversity. Women who have endured and overcome adversity offer invaluable advice to other women experiencing their own difficult life situations, even if the situations are different. Every woman has a story to offer, an experience to share—advice to pass on to those on the journey behind her.

Knowing someone who has survived hardship inspires us to believe that we too can overcome the difficulties in our own lives. Those who have emerged victorious chose to let the adversity deepen their character. They chose to let it make them better, rather than bitter. We discovered this important factor through interviewing hundreds of women: The choice one makes in the midst of hardship determines whether joy or bitterness becomes the core of who they are and how they live the rest of their lives.

Within just a few minutes of talking to a woman, her choice becomes evident. Bitter women are hard and uncomfortable to be with. Others radiate joy and peace. Sometimes their eyes just have a little unexplainable sparkle. These women seem to have made a choice in the midst of their adversity to let God use this experience in their life to grow their faith and character and to help others through similar situations—like the women in this chapter: Pat chose to use her painful experience of her husband's death to help other women in crisis. Betty learned to quit asking God "why?" and looked to Him for comfort through her difficult circumstances. Lorraine was able to comfort her daughter after her husband was killed in 9/11. And Jane chose to look at life as a temporary state, her body as a temporary dwelling for her spirit. She looks forward to her heavenly body and the incredible mansion that awaits her. From these choices all these women exude joy and peace.

They are women who have faced heartache and hardship, but they do not see themselves as victims of life. Instead, they are players in life who use their personal experiences to encourage others.

What are the hardships in your life right now? What positive choices can you make to redirect the hardships into something worthwhile?

In the midst of your hardship are you choosing to become a blessing to others or to be bitter? Write down your answer in a journal, and each week ask yourself this same question. Over time you will be able to see what attitudes you're developing.

Is there anyone in your life now enduring hardships? Pray for one thing you can do to help this person and do it.

Suggestions:
1. Seek out an older woman who has experienced a similar hardship to your own. Call her and ask her if she would be willing to share her experience with you. Let her know you need her wisdom and advice, and begin meeting with her on a regular basis.
2. Begin working with others to help them through their hardships. There are many organizations in the community and programs in churches needing volunteers. Pick up the phone and call one. Use your experience to help others.
3. Write Romans 8:28 on a card and tape it to your mirror or some other visible place: "And we know that in all things God works for the good of those who love him, who have been called according to his purpose." Read this verse often and look for the good things God is doing.

chapter two

where women walked . . .

through marriage

Sue

*When Sue said, "I forgive you," to her husband,
she meant it forever.*

Hunched under the belly of the cow she was milking, 13-year-old Sue heard the squeaky barn door open.

"Hey, Sue."

Sue's heart skipped a beat at the sound of her 16-year-old neighbor David's voice. "Hey," she answered softly. Streams of warm milk pulsed into the bucket at her feet.

"Do you want to go see a movie with me Friday night?"

Sue felt her face grow red. She glanced up to see if someone else was in the barn. Surely the popular high-school football stud wasn't asking *her* out. *But he's certainly not talking to the cow.* "Okay," Sue answered. She stood and wiped her milky hands on her slacks. "I have to ask my dad first," she said, trying to sound cool and calm.

"I already asked him," David said. He smiled.

Sue tripped over the milk bucket, spilling it onto the hay-covered ground. "What'd he say?" she asked, feeling miserably shy.

"He said it would be fine. I'll pick you up at six. See ya then."

As soon as David closed the door, Sue plopped down onto the

milking stool, resting her forehead against the cow's belly. *My first date!* She clapped her hand over her mouth, holding back a squeal of delight. *My friends aren't gonna believe this.*

The spark ignited in the barn that day grew into a flame of love. David and Sue dated each other exclusively throughout high school and college. Together they shared many firsts: their first date, their first trip to McDonalds, their first kiss, and then—their first child.

> *"If your spouse asks for your forgiveness, you need to give it like Christ forgave—absolutely! Your marriage will be better than you could ever imagine."*—Sue, 65

⟲⟳

Eighteen years old, pregnant, and head-over-heels in love, Sue married David two days before he started dental school. They had a baby girl and then two more children while David finished his schooling. Somehow during all this Sue managed to graduate from beauty school and worked to help David through school.

One day Sue snuggled up next to David on their tattered couch. They watched their three little children play on the small apartment floor around them. She looked up into the eyes of the man she loved and said, "I still can't believe that out of all the girls you could have had, you picked me."

"I didn't want anyone else," David said, wrapping his arms around her and kissing her gently on her forehead. "You were the best." He sighed. "I only wish I could give you more. But I promise you, as soon as I finish dental school and start my own practice, we'll buy a house and a car and we won't have to eat hamburger or canned fruit cocktail ever again."

"You know I don't care about any of that stuff," Sue said, resting her head on his strong shoulder. "I married the love of my life. I couldn't be happier." She closed her eyes, reveling in the blissful life they shared together.

After David graduated from dental school and served two years in the Air Force Dental Corps, he fulfilled the promises he had made to Sue. His successful dental practice helped them to buy the house of their dreams, buy a Cadillac, and even join the local country club. David and Sue rapidly moved from a life of poverty to a life of plenty. Suddenly, they were socializing with a different class of people—hobnobbing with society's elite. Sue loved dressing up and going to parties. But this lifestyle came at a high price.

The financial success and thrilling lifestyle they experienced blinded them to the warning flags and danger signs posted in front of them. David, who was working long hours to maintain his private dental practice, began frequenting a bar after work with his buddies—just to relax. Sue never dreamed this seemingly harmless habit would propel their relationship into a downward spiral toward destruction.

Because he didn't work on Wednesdays or weekends, David would go out regularly on Tuesdays and Fridays after work to party, arriving home around 6:30 in the evening. Over time this social gathering stretched into later hours. Occasionally he would stumble home during the wee hours of the morning. Sometimes Sue feared he might not come home at all.

Finally one night Sue snapped. David stumbled home late as usual, but this time a distraught, angry Sue confronted him. Grabbing his white button-down shirt, Sue ripped it open and began beating on his chest with both fists. She screamed, "Who do you think you are treating me like this? I can't take it anymore!"

David was so intoxicated he couldn't even react to her outrage. He mumbled something about being sorry.

"Sorry isn't enough. You and your friends act like slobbering idiots. Everyone sees you as the life of the party, but I think it's repulsive," Sue railed. The smell of alcohol emanating from his pores nauseated her.

David fell onto their bed without even changing his clothes and lapsed into a deep drunken sleep. Sue stared at him. *This is not the man I married. But what would I do if I left him? How would I provide for the kids?* Sue cried herself to sleep.

Nothing changed.

Six months later, their relationship reached a critical point. On their daughter's eighth birthday, David grabbed his jacket and headed out the front door.

"David, where are you going?" Sue asked, suspicious. "It's Sunday and it's only 10 in the morning." A sense of dread filled her and her mouth went dry. She tried to close the front door and redirect him to the kitchen.

"I'm just walking over to Stan's house for a few minutes," David said as he reopened the door and slipped his arms into the jacket sleeves.

"Today's Ann's birthday party. We're going ice-skating at one and then coming back here for cake—the Johnsons and the Robertsons are celebrating with us."

"I'll be back for ice-skating. Don't worry. I wouldn't forget my own daughter's birthday." David gave Sue a quick peck on the cheek, smiled his confident smile, and walked out the door.

David missed the ice-skating. Sue called him and pleaded with him to come home for cake. He didn't show up. For the children's sake, Sue put on her happy face and hosted a wonderful party. When David finally came home he found Sue in their bedroom packing her bags to leave.

"David, I can't take this anymore. You're not the man I married," Sue said as she folded her sweater and placed it on top of the other clothes in her suitcase. "You missed Ann's party today. I am so sick and tired of making up excuses for you. I don't know how I'm going to manage, but I'm getting out of here. The kids and I are leaving," Sue said resolutely.

"Sue, wait . . ." David bolted from the bedroom and out the front door. She heard him gagging and spitting as he vomited into the front bushes. She covered her mouth and closed her eyes, trying to shut out the image of who and what David had become. David returned to the bedroom, wiping the spit on his chin with his sleeve. "I know I'm an alcoholic. I know I need help. Will you give me one more chance?" he pleaded.

Sue sat down on the bed and began to cry. *Oh God, I want to help David, but I can't take this anymore. Help me to know what to do.* David lay down on the bed, the familiar smell of alcohol filling the room. As Sue looked at David and prayed, a vision of Christ suffering on the cross entered her mind. *If Jesus could painfully die on the cross and forgive humanity for killing Him, then I should follow His example and give David one more chance.*

> *"I kept a spiral notebook where I wrote everything I loved about David. When discouraged, I pulled out that notebook and read it. At first, it was hard to concentrate on these things, but this helped me remember how much I loved him."*—Sue

"David, you know I've started going to a women's Bible study. Well, I've been learning about Jesus Christ's sacrifice and what He did so that our sins would be forgiven. I guess if Jesus could die a painful death for me and forgive me of my sins, then I can try and forgive you. I love you, but you've got to get help."

David didn't change overnight. It took him one and a half years to quit drinking alcohol totally. He would quit, and then fall back. They would still attend the parties and he would try to just drink Coke. But sometimes, in a weak moment, he would lose his battle and the alcohol would win. During those times, Sue's heart splintered as she pled with God on David's behalf. She immersed herself in the Bible and talked to God constantly, continuing to ask Him to help her see David as the man He saw, not a man encumbered by his addiction.

After each relapse David would get back up and recommit himself to try again. His sincere efforts kept Sue's hope alive.

One morning, after recovering from a weekend binge, David told Sue they had to dispose of their bar. They had thousands of dollars' worth of alcohol. Together they opened up each bottle and poured it down the toilet.

As David struggled along, Sue's hopes were never depleted. She didn't give up.

Finally, after an annual fly-fishing trip with his buddies, David returned home with the usual puffy, red eyes and pale skin of a man who drank too much. "Sue, I can't do this on my own."

> *"I was keeping David in the guilt mode forever, instead of loving him as God loved him and forgiving him as God forgave him completely."—Sue*

He slowly climbed the stairs to their bedroom, but instead of collapsing into a deep slumber, he knelt at the foot of the bed, laid his head down on his folded hands, and wept. "Jesus," he cried out, "I can't change. I need Your help. I need You in my life. Please help me beat my alcoholism." Unexplainably, a sense of peace and calm swept over David and he felt another presence in the room. He looked around and didn't see anything, yet he felt a power surge through him, giving him the strength to change. To never take another drink. Filled with hope, he went downstairs to tell Sue about his supernatural experience.

"Sue, I committed my life to Christ just now and asked Him to help me never drink another drop of alcohol. I can't explain it but I felt like He was in the room with me. I know I can change; I can beat my alcoholism."

Sue cried as she clung to David. She saw a glimmer of the man he used to be.

Together, they started over. They made new friends and fell in love with each other all over again. David never drank another drop of alcohol. It was like the good old times!

But there was still one more thing Sue didn't know—one more iniquity requiring her absolute forgiveness. Driving to the mountains for a romantic weekend alone, they began talking about a friend who had confided in David that he had been unfaithful to his wife.

"He asked me if he should tell his wife. It happened a long time ago and never happened again. I don't know what to tell him. Do you think he should tell his wife?" David asked.

"Absolutely," Sue responded. "They will never enjoy the kind of marriage God intended for them until he confesses his affair to her and asks her for forgiveness. I mean, she doesn't need to know all the juicy details, but he needs to confess his sin."

When they arrived at the cabin, David, with trembling hands, turned off the car's ignition. He couldn't look at Sue for a long moment; then, finally, he faced her and, with his eyes filled with tears, softly said, "Sue, what you said about needing to confess our sins to enjoy the marriage God intended made me realize there is something I need to tell you. I have a confession to make. I've asked God for forgiveness, but I never thought I should ask you. One time when I was drunk I slept with another woman. I am sorry. I was so drunk, and it only happened one time. Can you forgive me for this?"

Stunned, Sue was speechless. *Lord, what do I do now? How do I handle this?* "David, I don't know what to say. I need to be alone." Tears streaming down her cheeks, she grabbed her Bible, hiked up the mountainside, and sat on a secluded rock. The warm summer sun beat down on her face as she looked up at the clear blue Colorado sky and sought God's comfort. "God, I feel so hurt and defiled. How could he do this to me? How many times do I have to forgive this man?" All alone, she cried out to God for hours.

Again she felt God tell her that she should forgive David just as Christ had forgiven her. Sue climbed down off that rock and went to find David in the cabin.

"David, I'm hurt beyond words. I didn't think I could forgive you for this, but with God's help I will try," she said.

The hurt took time to heal. Although Sue had said she forgave David, the pain and emotions would crop up and threaten to discourage her. During these times, she determined not to allow her mind to dwell on the pain. Whenever thoughts about David and his sin against her entered her mind, she would imagine Jesus standing at a chalkboard with junk scribbled all over it. Then Jesus would take an eraser and erase all the junk, making the chalkboard completely clean. Sue focused on the clean slate and kept reminding herself that the eraser had done its work.

"When my mind began to dwell on my own hurts, I would pray, 'Lord, You've forgiven David for this; help me to erase this from my mind.' "—Sue

Gradually, her hurt feelings faded. God promised to heal the hurt and He did.

Thirty years later, David still hasn't tasted a drop of alcohol. They work together in his dental practice and serve together in their church. On a scale of 1 to 10, Sue believes their marriage is a 15.

While she is sitting with a broad smile on her face, talking about David and her marriage today, the phone in the nearby home office rings. Sue slightly tilts her head to hear whose call she is ignoring.

But when she realizes the voice on the answering machine is David's, Sue bolts out of her chair and darts to answer the phone before he hangs up. "It's my honey!" she exclaims. And like a young girl, head-over-heels in love, she giggles and chats with her best friend and intimate companion of 42 years.

In Their Footsteps

"I stuck with my husband. Sometimes in pure joy, sometimes in just plain stubbornness, sometimes in hope, sometimes in despair, sometimes in anticipation, and sometimes in awesome dread, I stuck to the special man I chose to be my husband forever."
—*Anonymous woman married 51 years*

"You choose your partner for life and it's up to you both to make it work. No one is perfect, including you. So, with love, communication, and sometimes humor, walk yourselves through your problems with the Lord's help."
—*C., 71*

"It's your job to love him. It's God's job to change him."
—*Numerous women who filled out the survey*

"Practice patience and forgiveness in your marriage. When my husband was drinking excessively he asked the Lord to cause something to make him stop and, praise God, He did."
—*Anonymous, 86*

"Treat your husband with respect and honor. The respect and honor directed towards him reflects also on you."
—*Anonymous*

"Always remember you took your vows for a 'life' relationship. Don't try to change him. It will take much endurance and unselfishness, but as the days, weeks, months, and years go on, a respect for him will happen. This will pay rich dividends!"
—*Shirley, 67*

Martha

*Once Martha stopped trying to control her
husband and focused on getting to know him,
she began loving him more than ever.*

Martha adjusted the rearview mirror to glance at herself before getting
out of her car. *Ugh! I can't wait to take a shower. Nine hours in a car with
your head mashed against the headrest sure does a number on your hair*,
she thought. She stepped out of the car, stretched, and then tried to
straighten out her sweater and slacks to make herself somewhat pre-
sentable for her friend Trisha. *At least Paul is hundreds of miles away and
won't see me like this.*

Martha rang the doorbell. As the door opened, Martha's heart
skipped a beat and her jaw dropped.

"Hi, Mar! Surprise!" Paul said with a grin. Then, before she could
utter a word, a bright flash blinded her—a camera on a tripod had just
captured her rumpled image forever.

"Paul!" Martha said, shaking her head and rubbing her eyes, trying
to make sense out of the situation. "What are you doing here? Where's
Trisha? Why are you wearing a tux?" Even while she uttered those
words, realization of what he was up to dawned in her mind. *Oh my*

gosh, he's going to ask me to marry him! Oh my goodness, Lord. I never dreamed this is how it would happen.

She feigned a smile but cringed inside, knowing how awful she must look.

"Trisha said I could borrow her place this evening. I've made you dinner. Come on in," Paul said as he stepped aside and the warm glow of candles welcomed her into her friend's home.

"Uh, sure," Martha said as she tried to control the panic she felt rising inside her. "Sorry I am such a mess. It's been a long drive. I think I'd better go freshen up a bit."

Martha rushed to the bathroom, closed the door, and sat down on the edge of the tub. *Why do I feel like the fattened calf that's about to be slaughtered?* she wondered. *We've talked about marriage. I just wish I had known he was planning this. What am I going to say?*

"Lord," she prayed, "I believe this is the man you want me to marry. I'm in love with him. If you don't want me to marry this man, then please make me sick to my stomach." She waited . . . nothing. Her stomach felt fine. "Okay, Lord, I'm going to say yes."

> *"Control is all about having my way. Ultimately, all I cared about was myself."—Martha, 51*

ᕦᕤ

Somewhere between the steak and baked potato, Paul reached across the table, held Martha's hand, and asked her to marry him. Of course, she said, "Yes."

Early one beautiful sunny Saturday a few years into their marriage, Martha stood at the kitchen window and thought, *Marriage is a breeze. Whoever thought marriage was hard didn't marry someone as easy to get along with as Paul.*

Martha grabbed his favorite mug from the shelf, filled it up with freshly brewed hot tea, and delivered it to him in bed. "Hey, sleepy-head, wake up. It's a beautiful day. Why don't we pack a picnic and go for a hike?"

Paul pulled the pillow over his head, grunted something unintelligible, and rolled over to go back to sleep.

"Oh, come on, hon. Get up, let's get going. I've planned a full day."

"How 'bout I sleep a little longer. Then we'll talk about our day," Paul mumbled.

"Well, okay, but not too long because I want to show you a couch I fell in love with for our living room. I was also hoping to get some chores done in the yard sometime today. Oh, and I told the Langes we would join them for dinner. I thought it would be fun to try that new Mexican restaurant downtown and then go see a movie."

"But it's Saturday. Can't we just kick back and relax?"

"Are you kidding? Don't be lazy. That's what Saturday is for. Pack it full with fun."

"All right, just give me 30 more minutes," pleaded Paul.

By the time Paul wandered into the kitchen, Martha was busily packing a picnic. As soon as he'd eaten breakfast, she grabbed his hand and pulled him out the door. "Come on. I've got to show you this couch before someone else buys it. It's perfect. You're going to be thrilled."

Paul and Martha drove to the nearby furniture store, Martha bursting with excitement over the couch she'd been searching for and finally found. Inside the store, she took Paul's hand and dragged him to the display. "There it is; don't you just love it?" she asked. She pointed to a navy, rust, and cream-colored, flame-stitched Queen Anne sofa. "This is totally in. It's what all the expensive homes have, but this one is less expensive. It's such a deal! Isn't it great?"

A look of confusion crossed Paul's face. "Mar, do you really like it?"

"Like it? I love it. Don't you?"

"I think that's the ugliest couch I've ever seen," Paul confessed.

Martha couldn't believe he didn't like it. Smiling at Paul she thought, *You really don't know anything about decorating. I mean, look at the furniture you brought into our marriage, like that ugly plastic Coca-Cola lamp that looks like it should be hanging over a pool table in some cheap bar!* Biting her tongue and still smiling, she said, "But it's perfect!

It's the right colors and will look great in our living room. Don't worry. It'll grow on you."

Paul didn't say anything more about the couch. Martha realized, much to her dismay, that her husband did indeed have certain opinions about furniture style, and for the rest of the day she fumed inside because she knew she wasn't going to get her dream couch after all.

Seven years and two kids later, Paul decided to enter a seminary and earn a degree in counseling. Part of the requirement to complete the program involved participating in marriage counseling with Martha. Martha thought it would be great fun and a good learning experience. Besides, they had a "great marriage." They had done everything "right." They enjoyed weekly date nights, led a Bible study together, and rarely argued. It would be a breeze.

> *"You know you're controlling if, whenever your husband is driving, you neurotically look over your shoulder to see if any cars are coming prior to him switching lanes."*
> —*Martha*

During their first session with the counselor, they answered such typical questions as how long they'd been married and how many kids they had. Then the counselor asked Paul, "How do you feel about being married to Martha?"

Paul paused for a minute to think before answering.

"Well, I feel like I married a strong-willed, wild stallion who's taking me on a ride and I have no control over where we're going. I don't know what to do with her."

Martha stared at Paul, completely floored by his response!

"Wow, I had no idea he felt this way; he's never said anything like that before," was all Martha could manage to say. Over the next several weeks Paul's words slowly sank in and Martha realized a cooperative spirit did not exist between them. She had all the opinions and made all the plans. That's why being married to Paul was so easy—she pretty much got whatever she wanted.

These counseling sessions opened up a new chapter in their married life. Martha began to see her tendency to control while Paul began to learn to express his thoughts and feelings.

At times Martha felt hopeless because her urge to control had been with her as long as she could remember. Seeing how this aspect of her personality hurt her relationship with Paul, she wanted to change. But habits are hard to change—impossible, Martha felt, to change on her own. She needed help from God, so she asked Him to change her.

> *"You need to be your husband's number-one fan. Typically, men don't receive much praise—so be quick to encourage."*
> *—Martha*

After a year of intense praying and counseling, Martha began to see success in resisting her urge to control.

For example, one summer day she and Paul were meeting friends from Texas at the beach. Having been raised in the South, Martha was familiar with the customs of Southerners. She just knew their friends would be dressed to the hilt. Paul came out wearing a plaid shirt and royal blue shorts that she had given him for the occasion. But in her opinion his outfit wasn't complete.

"Aren't you going to wear a belt?" she blurted out.

"I don't want to wear a belt," Paul firmly answered. (He was learning to express his opinions and communicate his desires, even if it meant conflict with Martha.)

"But your outfit would look so much more complete with a belt."

"I don't like wearing belts. We're going to the beach, and I don't want to wear a belt at the beach."

"Can't you just wear it for me? Please, I want you to look nice today," Martha begged.

Paul stomped back into the house, angrily put on a belt, stomped back to the car, slammed the door shut, and drove silently toward their destination. During their tense, uncomfortably quiet drive, Martha had time to think. *Why do I care so much about Paul's appearance?* The truth hit her like a hammer, and it hurt.

"Paul," Martha quietly said, "I'm sorry. I feel so shallow. I realize I wanted you to wear a belt because ultimately, I wanted you to make me look good." Through her tears Martha continued, "I truly thought that if you didn't have a belt on to complete your outfit, then my friends would think I was married to a man who didn't know how to dress—and that wouldn't make me look good. I am so sorry."

> *"If you control your husband, then you will never find out who he really is. If you want to find out his likes and dislikes, you've got to ask him."—Martha*

Paul gently squeezed her hand and said, "Thanks for saying that, Mar. I love you. I'll wear the silly belt." Martha felt so grateful for Paul's gracious response, but the rest of the day, as she looked at him, that silly belt was a constant reminder of her own selfish desire for him to make her look good. But it was also a reminder of how far she had come in recognizing her urge to control and her success in conquering this urge.

Today, after 21 years of marriage, Paul and Martha have developed strategies to break the control cycle. When Martha feels the urge to control Paul, she automatically asks herself, "Why?" She questions her heart's motives. "If it's more about me, or what people will think about me, then I know my motives are probably wrong."

Martha still faces new challenges in not being able to control life. Paul was recently diagnosed with a rare form of cancer. Once again, Martha has had to let go of control and lean on God heavily! After a successful surgery, Paul's future is still unsure, but together, they are taking this unpredictable ride and letting God hold the reins.

In Their Footsteps

"Communicate. Ask your husband questions. For too long I tried to guess. I played the detective instead of just asking him, 'What can I do for you today?'"
                                        —*Sande, 62, married 41 years*

"Make your husband your very best friend."
                                        —*Connie, 57*

"Believe in your husband."
                                        —*Jan, 58*

"Be understanding with your husband. No one person is always right."
                                        —*Mary Ann, 75, married for 55 years*

"Honor him with respect. Praise him. Men are little boys who love praise no matter their position in life."
                                        —*Anonymous, 66*

"Listen, listen, listen, every day. Know and believe he is there for you as you are for him."
                                        —*Sue, 59*

"Be less critical and more caring, loving, and understanding."
                                        —*Anonymous, 65*

"I realized I had left everything I loved about him at the altar when we got married. I saw it as my task to change him to be more like me. In the process of doing this, I destroyed his ego, his sense of worth. My heart was nothing but critical, and I finally saw myself for what I was."
                                        —*Debbie, 52*

Pat

*Keeping romance alive in marriage is difficult, especially
with little people running around. Pat found that
planning romantic times away helped to keep the fire
of passion burning bright in her marriage.*

Pat and Jeff held hands as they peered into their two sons' bedrooms.

"They're sound asleep," whispered Pat. She felt a little chilly creeping around the house in her teeny-weeny bright pink bikini.

"Finally," whispered Jeff as he gently pulled Pat out the back door toward the hot tub he'd recently installed on their deck.

The balmy air of a June night and the stars sparkling brilliantly in the clear sky made for a perfect night of romance. They settled into the warm water of the tub and things quickly started to heat up. (Not the water in the hot tub.)

"Jeff," Pat paused, "do you think we should be careful? I don't want to get pregnant. Brent is only eight months old."

"Nah. Hot water kills sperm. Besides, you're breast-feeding."

Nine months later to the day, Pat and Jeff welcomed bouncing nine-pound, two-and-a-half-ounce son Blake into the world.

Needless to say, with three boys ranging from newborn to nine years old, spontaneous romantic nights in the hot tub became less frequent. Pat found it hard to relax with a new baby constantly needing attention. Even when the baby was asleep she still worried about her older sleepwalking son—never knowing when or where he would appear. Most of her waking hours, someone was tugging or sucking on her, making it even more difficult to feel sexy and desirable at the end of the day. To top it all off, constant fatigue kept her sexual desire to a minimum. Yet Pat felt guilty that she wasn't making intimacy with her husband a priority. He always seemed to be in the background of everything else going on in the house.

One day Jeff came up with a great idea. While Pat sat on the couch nursing the baby and the two other boys played around her in the family room, Jeff slipped her a little handwritten note that said, "How about an appointment a little later?" Seeing the desire in his eyes Pat nodded her head yes. At the moment she wasn't feeling too sexy, but anticipating a time later that evening when the boys were all asleep gave her something to look forward to. This became their method of communicating with each other about their individual needs for intimate times. They enjoyed slipping each other little notes asking for an appointment and then planning and anticipating that romantic time.

> *"We also would plan an early morning rendezvous. We're both early birds, so we enjoyed waking up before the kids and spending intimate time with each other."—Pat, 57*

Sometimes they would wrap up their notes detailing a planned getaway and give them to each other for Christmas or Valentine's Day.

Then life threw some hard stuff at them—stuff that causes a high percentage of marriages to end in divorce. Their son Blake, at the precious age of three, contracted meningitis and suddenly died. The pain and grief they experienced was beyond words. They floundered, trying to comprehend the senseless loss of their child. At times Pat felt like she couldn't make her marriage work with Jeff. It was just too hard.

In Their

"When you marry you must ma
when you begin having children,
the most important person in you
spend most of your days and hou
a house . . . and maybe holding a
—*Anonymous, (*

"One time when I was on a trip
sonal, passionate message on his
him and loved him. When he pic
ately kissed me. He loved my me
over on a deserted road; we cou
other."
—*Anonymous,*

"Be attentive to your husband w
preoccupied with other things ar
that what he says is not importar
the two of you to be alone."
—*Jane, 59*

"I've tried to keep romance and
to do the things that will please
of effort on my part. I also try to
a few minutes to do what he wan
of the basketball game he's watch
he wants to share it with somebo
—*Pat, 72, ma*

Then Jeff asked her, "What would Blake think if we broke up this family?" Pat knew Jeff was right.

"I could never break up this family," Pat responded through her tears. "Blake would hate that." They would make it, no matter what.

Shortly after their son's death, Pat suffered a miscarriage. Unable to conceive another child, she and Jeff decided to adopt. They were selected to be the parents of a beautiful infant girl. She helped them through their grief, and slowly the pain eased a bit. They loved children so much and wanted another, so within a few years they adopted another baby girl.

> *"Jeff's day off is Tuesday, so that's our day together. We always have lunch together and we'll have a little time with the door closed too."—Pat*

As their family grew, Pat and Jeff's time together shrank. It became more important than ever to plan that precious time alone. So they began to schedule a getaway once or twice a year. They didn't have to go anywhere exotic, just away from the children. When they were low on cash they would ask their parents to baby-sit. Sometimes they traded baby-sitting with friends. Sometimes they saved up their money and paid a sitter. Whatever it took, they made this time away happen. Pat always came back feeling rejuvenated as a mom and reconnected to Jeff.

Now that Pat's girls are teenagers, it doesn't mean they're any less demanding of her time, energy, and attention. More than ever she feels the need to plan getaways with Jeff.

Not long ago they planned a romantic weekend away that went a little awry. Pat packed the car and the moment Jeff arrived home, they said good-bye to the girls and drove off into the sunset.

"Did you pack the snack sack?" Jeff asked.

"Of course," Pat said as she pulled out the familiar pack they always take on their getaways filled with junk food like Chex Mix, potato chips, and sweets—unhealthy, yummy junk they never eat at home.

"Got any chocolates in there?" Jeff asked with a wide grin.

"Do I have chocolates! Do
filled?"

They spent their driving
kids. Unfortunately, on this tr
both came down with the sto
end hugging the porcelain r
dampen their love. They retu
looking forward even more to

"We've weathered the wor

> "E-mail is great. You can
> always send your
> husband sweet e-mails
> during the day."—Pat

∾

on a more serious note, do wh
husband; even though the log

Marriage Summary

∾

"In the name of God, I take you to be my husband,
to have and to hold from this day forward,
for better or worse, for richer or poorer,
in sickness and in health, to love and to cherish
until we are parted by death.
This is my solemn vow."

Beautiful young brides face their husbands at the altar, dizzy with emotions as they pledge this vow. Most young brides don't have a clue what they are signing up for—they just know their knight in shining armor is about to sweep them away on a white horse for a happily-ever-after life. Flushed and giddy with excitement, they say, "I do." But when the honeymoon ends and the reality of marriage begins, the confused bride thinks, "So this is it?"

Some relationships encounter more difficulties than others, but for everyone, marriage takes hard work and commitment through good times and bad. The women we interviewed almost unanimously felt that perseverance through the hard times was worth it.

Martha eventually took her focus off her husband's flaws and realized she had the responsibility for changing her own attitudes and actions. Sue forgave her husband again and again, persevering through his addiction. And Pat, by planning romantic getaways, makes alone time with her husband a high priority in their marriage.

Most of all, their determination to uphold their sacred and solemn marital vows has been rewarded with marriages that remain intact and stronger than ever.

What are the struggles in your marriage? What are the core issues? In what ways are you responsible for contributing to the problem?

What are the four most important elements to making a marriage strong and enduring? Which of these does your marriage have? Which can you work on to strengthen from your own choices and attitudes?

List three marriages you know that are strong and enduring. What qualities do the individuals bring to these marriages that make them so?

Suggestions:
1. Have a potluck luncheon with several of your friends and some older women who have solid marriages. Make "marriage" the theme of the luncheon and ask the older women to pass along their suggestions and wisdom for making a marriage strong and enduring. Ask them how they've learned to respect their husbands.
2. Have a private journal into which you write daily, or at minimum weekly, the positive qualities you see in your husband. Praise him in the journal for specific ways that he builds your marriage. (Do not put anything negative in this journal.) When he gets on your nerves or does something that makes you angry, read this journal and remember what kind of man you are married to.
3. Also write prayers for your marriage in this journal.
4. Plan a romantic getaway for the two of you. Be creative; it doesn't have to be costly.
5. Buy a journal to write love notes to each other in. Pass it back and forth between the two of you.

chapter three

where women walked . . .

as mothers

Eileen

*Trying to be a perfect mom and raise perfect children
in an imperfect world can turn any mother into a
basket case. Eileen, the perennial wanna-be super
mom, finally learned to relax and trust God with
her kids, giving her a serious case of perfect peace.*

Eileen blew the whistle hanging around her neck and hollered, "Stop!
All of you. Freeze. What just happened out there?"

The group of 10-year-old boys stopped and stared at her, completely confused. The soccer ball hadn't even rolled out of bounds.

"Mom," her son Luke said, "what are you talking about?"

"I saw some very inappropriate behavior and I want to talk about
it. Does anyone want to tell me what went wrong?"

Again, the boys stared blankly at Eileen, their soccer coach and a
single mom, who knew nothing about soccer.

"I'll tell you what went wrong. David made a great pass to Erik, and
no one praised him for it. You need to support each other. You're a
team! Encourage each other." She clapped her hands. "Okay, let's play."

As they wrapped up practice, Eileen noticed David and Erik teas-
ing Luke about an easy goal he had missed. Luke was trying to laugh it

off but Eileen knew that inside, he felt embarrassed and hurt by the others laughing at him. *Those two boys are trouble. I definitely don't want Luke hanging out with them,* she thought as she put the last soccer ball into the net bag. *But Chris seems pretty nice. He's respectful to me, he's nice to the other kids, and he listens well. I'll have to invite him over to play with Luke this weekend.*

> *"I believed my children's outcome was totally dependent on me. Therefore, I alone had the total overwhelming responsibility for molding and shaping them."*
> —*Eileen, 51*

Coaching her son's soccer team was a brilliant idea. Even though she knew nothing about soccer, she could get to know the kids and see which ones behaved appropriately. Then she could make sure her children made friends with the right kids, not the troublemakers. *I know my kids have to be in the world, but I'm sure going to protect them from all the bad stuff I can.*

Driving home from soccer practice with Luke, Eileen picked up her 13-year-old daughter, Sarah, from school and made a quick stop at the health food store. "We need to get a few things for tomorrow. There's a party at Luke's school but I don't want him eating all that sugar they hand out. Let's find a few healthy snacks for him to take to eat instead," Eileen said.

While shopping, Sarah moped around the store, showing little interest in any kind of conversation. "Sarah, what's wrong?" Eileen asked. "You seem upset about something."

Sarah picked up a box of couscous and turned it over and over in her hands. She sighed. "Mr. O'Neal made me stay in the classroom during lunch today because I was talking with Kathy during class." She slammed the box back on the shelf. "Class was sooo boring."

"Do you want me to give him a call?" Eileen asked, as she read the label on the sesame candy she considered purchasing for Luke's party.

"No way, Mom. That just makes things worse." Sarah crossed her arms and turned away. "I hate it when you call my teachers."

"Well, I think he should know you're bored in his class. You need more of a challenge. It seems like he should be able to do something to keep you more interested."

Sarah just rolled her eyes and wandered away from her mom.

That evening Eileen fixed her kids the usual vegetarian dinner, helped them with their homework, and read books to them until bedtime. After kissing them each she went to bed. But sleep hung back, kept at bay by her busy mind processing thoughts a million miles a minute. She did not have time to fit rest and relaxation into her busy schedule. Instead, she planned.

I'll need to arrange a play date for Luke and Chris. No watching television or videos at my house! No couch potatoes here! I'll take them to get some good outdoor exercise—swimming! I'll call Sarah's science teacher tomorrow morning, leave a message, and perhaps he'll call during lunch. That would work out perfect with . . .

Eileen's thoughts spun and planned every detail of the next few days. After a couple of hours, she finally slept.

Eileen's life had whizzed along mostly as she ordered. She re-met Mark, a high school acquaintance and self-proclaimed bachelor for life. They married and had two children together, sending Eileen down the road of trying to be the perfect mother and wife. Like a ball in a pinball machine, she bounced from circumstance to circumstance, from event to event. She tried to be everything to everybody.

Unfortunately, her controlled world began to unravel when her daughter hit the turbulent teen years. Eileen wanted desperately to rein Sarah back into the safety and security of the life she had worked so hard to create. Nothing she tried worked. The situation grew worse, so Eileen sought family counseling.

After the initial interview, the counselor pulled Eileen aside and said, "Eileen, the kids are not the problem. You are the problem. You must stop controlling everything."

"But I'm only trying to protect them," Eileen protested.

The counselor looked at Eileen with compassion. "I know. But by protecting them you aren't training them to handle situations on their own. You aren't their rescue helicopter who needs to swoop in and take care of everything. You need to let your children go."

During this time Eileen also hungered for spiritual growth and community in her life and in the lives of her children. So she began searching for a church. She visited all sorts of churches but none satisfied the growing need inside her. One day Eileen met a lovely woman who invited her to a women's Bible study. When Eileen walked into the room filled with friendly young women, she literally felt a peace and a comfortable presence in the room.

> *"Instead of rescuing my children from every circumstance, I try to help them develop the tools they need to handle whatever comes their way."—Eileen*

There's so much love, comfort, and a sense of truth here, she thought. *I've tried so many different churches and religions, but this is different; I feel like I just walked into my home after being gone for so long.* Overcome with a sense of relief, Eileen cried, thinking, *I'm finally home.*

Not long after, she made another choice that changed her life forever. While attending the Bible study she learned more about Jesus Christ and how she could have a personal relationship with Him. Sitting in the sanctuary of this church, she said to God, "Okay, Jesus, You know all the stuff I have believed over the years, but I'm going to choose You and You alone." Eileen then put her life into hands she really trusted—the hands of a loving God. For the first time, she gave up the tremendous burden she carried—the burden of feeling totally responsible for her children and their lives. Instead, she began trusting God to take care of them.

Looking back, Eileen realizes she hadn't been allowing her children to learn their own lessons. "The pressure I felt to protect and provide for my kids was so overwhelming." Over time her parenting style changed, not so much in *what* she did, but *why* she did what she did.

The realization that a loving God was in control of every detail of her life and her children's lives gave her tremendous freedom and peace.

"I now realize I am merely a steward for the Lord, who loves my children more than I do, and He has a much better plan for them. I see myself as a facilitator of that plan."

She is still careful about what Luke and Sarah eat, what they watch, and what they listen to, but her motivation is no longer fear and the desire to control their lives. "I think, so what if they eat a few Oreos with orange cream in the middle? It won't kill them."

Now, when her two children, who still live at home, return from school complaining about a teacher or a difficult situation, she doesn't immediately take charge and fix their problems for them. Instead, she asks, "What are your choices? Which do you think is the best choice? What are you going to do to help this situation?" Eileen has developed such a deep trust in God for her children's well-being that she can now release her own control.

> *"I was the mother lion. You just didn't mess with my kids. Now I know my kids are going to get messed with. The best thing I can do is teach them to deal with it."*
> *—Eileen*

The result? She is now enabling her children to handle difficult circumstances on their own.

Eileen radiates a true sense of peace and calm. She is no longer an anxious and stressed-out mom. "I used to be a whirling dervish, constantly at work, nonstop, going, going, going, doing, doing, doing." Eileen laughs at her old self. "Now I'm more about *being*. Who I am *being* for my kids, not what I am *doing* for them."

Eileen's trust in God and her love for her family provide an awesome example of how God works in the lives of mothers willing to trust and surrender control to Him.

"Letting go of the need to control and putting trust in an almighty, loving God brings peace." Eileen knows from firsthand experience.

In Their Footsteps

"Be selective of the activities in which you become involved so that you can spend quality time with your little ones."
— *JoAnn, 67, who also expressed the need for mothers to make time for prayer in life*

"Some people refer to being a mom as the most important job you'll ever have. I don't think being a mom is like a job at all, because you don't work your way up any ladder, and you don't gain more responsibility through time. I think it's the opposite. When you become a mom, you're handed your biggest responsibility, BANG, right at the beginning. The emotional and physical demands are the highest for about the first 15 years. A good mom works herself out of a job. The precious relationship continues through life, but you have to let go of the responsibility and let your children live independently of you, and you independently of them."
— *Elizabeth, 76*

"Show them the joy of life and how important they are to you."
— *Anonymous, 61, who also says she wishes she had not shouldered so much responsibility for the family, home, and relationships alone*

"Children are the most precious, and the most frustrating, creatures on earth. They shrink your world to four walls, reduce your mind to mush, and make you act as young as they are . . . without losing any energy. Their job is to push the envelope, to find the boundaries, to push you as the nearest, handiest boundary. They will do this until they move out of the home and you cry for months because they are gone. So while you have them, love them and praise them. Emphasize the positive, teach them love and acceptance and fun, and how to try their hardest."
— *T. S., 55*

Barbara

Staying at home with small kids is challenging even on the best of days. Barbara's unique circumstances made her job as a mom especially demanding. Yet in the chaos of her life, she realized she had a choice to make. She could: A) scream loudly, pull her hair out, and run away without looking back or B) enjoy the irreplaceable moments and depend on God for her ability as a mom. She chose to enjoy the moments.

"Mom, can I have more juice?"

"Mommy, this chicken is icky."

"Mom, tell Sarah to stop touching me."

A never-ending barrage of mealtime requests bombarded Barbara. Her four children, David, an energy-filled three-year-old, Sarah, a mischievous two-year-old, and the one-year-old twins, Christina and Julia, took more effort than she'd ever thought possible. *Whoever thinks staying at home with children is not a "real job" obviously never tried it.*

Barbara bustled about the kitchen, wishing she had a few minutes to herself. Certainly she needed more rest. She pressed her fingers to her eyes, trying to push away the blurriness that had plagued her for the past few days. *I spend too much time in this kitchen,* she thought.

She sighed, opened the refrigerator, and took out the juice pitcher. Mechanically, she poured apple juice into a sippy cup she could hardly see. As she sank into a chair, all the clamor faded as she attempted to focus on the faces of her children.

Something is wrong. Something is very, very wrong, she thought, her heart pounding. Then, it came to her. *Please, God, don't let it be* that.

As a teenager, she had been diagnosed with a chronic eye disease. Doctors told her it could flare up again if the scar tissue behind her eyes shifted. Before she was married, she had a short period in which her vision had become slightly impaired, but her sight went quickly back to normal. Now it felt like someone was holding something directly in front of her, blocking her central vision. With her peripheral vision she could see fine, *but I can't see the faces of my children,* she thought, dumbfounded.

Maybe it will get better if I just get a good night's sleep, she told herself as she hurried the kids into their pajamas.

In the morning it was no better. Her husband, Richard, a pediatrician, wrapped her in his arms after she told him about it. "It's okay, Barb. We'll do whatever needs to be done to fix the problem."

Richard stayed true to his promise. Together they visited numerous specialists all over the country. Yet no one had any answers. Their comments all sounded the same.

"There is nothing that can be done."

"This is a very rare type of blindness and we don't know too much about it."

"There is a slim chance the scar tissue could shift again and your vision would be restored. But restoration is so rare that we wouldn't want you to get your hopes up."

In between her visits to eye specialists, Barbara began the arduous task of adjusting to her disability. Her husband, establishing his pediatric practice, often had to put in 70 hours per week. She didn't want to add to his stress by troubling him with her problems, so she set out to do everything alone.

"I am feeling so frustrated," she said one night to her older friend Liz. "Every day I'm discovering how much I can't do. I can't drive. I can't shop for anything—not even a bra! I can't take the children anywhere. I can't read them stories."

It felt good to have someone to share her frustrations with. Liz was a great encourager, always helping Barbara stay positive. With Liz motivating her, Barbara made up her mind to get creative and find new things she could do with the kids, rather than dwell on what she couldn't do any more.

Soon Barbara began to see ways to make her condensed, limited world a more fun and manageable place to be. She memorized every part of her house so she could move about with ease, completing chores and caring for her children. She accepted the kind offers from neighbors and friends who took her children to the park or community swimming pool. When fun for the children was not possible away from home, she brought fun inside—especially in the long evening hours when Richard tended to pediatric emergencies. They made masks from paper bags and corn husks. They made vegetables into funny ink-stamp faces. They baked cookies and decorated them. And sometimes they even sat on the floor eating sticky pancake picnic dinners. It was simple stuff, but Barbara learned fast that it doesn't take much to entertain small children.

Even so, life was not easy. Barbara often felt like a single mom, carrying most of the load at home with the children by herself. At night she would fall into bed, exhausted from taking care of the kids all day.

Daily she prayed for God to give her the strength and ingenuity to meet her unique challenges. *Lord, help me to handle all the situations I will face today. Help me to choose to enjoy what I do have and not wallow in the difficult circumstances.*

One day, about sixth months into her blindness, Barbara's husband turned to her while putting groceries away. "Barb, have you ever prayed that God would heal you?"

She thought a moment. "Well, I guess not," she answered. "I always pray that He'll give me strength."

"Healing is the first thing I'd have prayed for," Richard said, sticking the milk into the fridge.

Barbara considered her husband's suggestion. The next morning she incorporated it into her daily prayers. "Father, please heal me."

Two years later, God answered her prayers, and her vision slowly returned.

One afternoon while Barbara and the kids picnicked at a park, David began testing his mommy's newly restored eyesight—his new favorite pastime. "Mommy, can you see this?" he said holding up a big red ball in front of her.

"Yes, sweetie," she laughed. "But more important, now I can see this," she said touching his innocent little face. As he climbed up into her lap, her eyes drank in his features and her heart leapt with gratefulness.

> *"We need to remember that God says, 'I AM.' Not 'I was' or 'I will be.' We are called to be aware of Him in the now—to live with Him in the now!"*—Barbara

Ꮼ᎐

Now Barbara looks back on those years with fond memories. Her motto has become "Life is messy," and those years in her life were particularly messy. "You see," laughs Barbara, "we all need to know life rarely goes as planned." Especially if you happen to be a mom of young children." To illustrate her conviction she holds up a faded, food-stained poster of a pudgy toddler dumping a bowl of spaghetti over his head. Psalm 118:24 is printed at the bottom of the poster. It says, "This is the day the LORD has made; let us rejoice and be glad in it."

Looking at the mess portrayed by the poster, Barbara continues, "This became my verse as I raised my kids. I knew I had to make a choice to enjoy the moment, or go crazy and run away from home."

Today, with all her children grown and out of the house, Barbara spends a lot of time mentoring young mothers in her church. She encourages these stay-at-home moms by reminding them that parenting is a tough job, which from the outside can look easy. "We know that's not true," she tells them. "Until you're wearing 'mom' shoes you can't begin to understand the challenges that moms face while caring for needy, small children 24 hours a day. It's fatiguing, not very rewarding, and quite unpleasant at times. But moms need to remember that they'll miss out on a whole lot if all they are doing is waiting for their kids to get older."

Barbara enthusiastically encourages moms of young children, "Don't be so bothered by the mess in your house or how your big plans fall apart for the day. Remember that each day has been given to us by the Lord and He wants us to cherish it."

In Their Footsteps

"Looking back, it seems like I was so anticipating the times when my husband would be through with medical school, our son would be potty trained, and our daughter would sleep through the night. I just wanted to hurry into the next stage. There are great, wonderful things about each stage of life. Look for them and appreciate them. Anticipation is great if it doesn't rob you of the present."
　　　—*Eulalie, 55*

"There is stress when children are young, but learn to enjoy each day—every day, no matter what stage."
　　　—*Jan, 59*

"As I was the youngest of 10 children and living on a farm, not close to the city or neighbors, I didn't have the privilege of baby-sitting. So with my children I learned mostly by trial and error! However, the Lord is a patient teacher and He taught me daily as there were times I cried with the babies! In those hours I learned much by listening to older mothers, who had raised their children and taught them from a very young age to love Jesus."
　　　—*Shirley, 66*

"Enjoy them while they are young and don't worry about every little thing. Look at the BIG picture, not at every action in a day."
　　　—*Dawn, 57*

Edith

*As a little girl, Edith dreamed of getting married and
having children. Things seemed to be going her way after she
married a man she adored and they had three beautiful
children. When a painful divorce shattered her dreams,
Edith felt scared and hopeless about her future. But slowly,
she chose to allow God to rebuild her life, creating new
dreams for her and her children.*

Hearing the loudspeaker announce it was time to board the plane,
Edith's heart started drumming a battle beat. Swallowing hard, she
stood up and prodded her three children toward the gate. For the first
time since her divorce, her children were flying to Missouri to visit their
father.

After good-bye hugs, the children happily scurried down the board-
ing ramp, loudly calling, "Bye, Mommy." Giving last-minute admon-
ishments Edith hollered back, "Be good . . . Brush your teeth . . . No
fighting on the plane!"

The second they were out of sight, her brave front dissolved and she
let out a broken sob. Fumbling through her purse for a tissue, she
slowly made her way to a secluded seat where she could watch their

plane take off. As the plane disappeared into the sky, her throat felt tight. A feeling of utter desperation swept through her body. With tears streaming down her face, she realized again just how shattered her dreams had become.

"It wasn't supposed to be like this," she whispered to herself while staring at the empty sky. As busy people bustled by her, Edith thought about her simple childhood dream to be a mother and raise her children with a man she deeply loved. As she fished for another tissue, her mind strayed to the previous five painful years of a long separation that ended in divorce.

> *"I thought I would go insane watching my precious babies get on a plane without me. I was coming unglued."—Edith, 70*

∾

The years of separation had dragged on for what seemed like forever to Edith. To ease her pain and pass the time, Edith had taken the children to Ohio to visit her parents whenever she could. Staring blankly out the big airport window, Edith remembered one Sunday morning during an Ohio visit when she went to church with her mother. Walking through the double white doors of the small country church, holding on to the arm of her mother, Edith immediately felt at home. She attended Bible class that morning. The lesson, as well as the kind people, filled her with a sense of security. Driving home later that morning Edith felt a reassurance in her spirit. "Mama," she said with a faint smile, "I can feel God is with me. In this big mess of my life, He is still with me."

"Yes. He is, sweetheart." Her mother nodded with conviction.

Wiping the tears from her face Edith couldn't help but smile as she thought about how God had proven Himself faithful over and over again during those dark days. Her thoughts immediately skipped to another Ohio trip when God again proved Himself trustworthy. She had been driving down a long stretch of two-lane highway early one morning in her red station wagon. As she cruised down the highway, her thoughts were preoccupied with the children and finances. She simply didn't see the red light and went straight through it. The moment she crossed underneath the light, she saw something out of the corner of her eye hurtling with great force behind her back tires. Then a powerful blast of a horn rang in her ears. As she looked over her shoulder she saw a semi truck rushing by just inches away from the back of her car.

With the sound of the horn echoing through her mind, Edith pulled her car over. Panting, she thought, *Okay, Lord, any other dummy would have been smeared across the road—but not me. You must really want me to live.*

Convinced after that moment that God had a purpose for her broken life, Edith began to slowly accept that her old dreams were gone. And she began realizing God could help her mold new dreams and a new life. But this wasn't easy.

Edith stood up from her seat in the airport and began making her way down the concourse, her thoughts churning. *It is such a struggle for me to totally trust God with my life and the lives of my kids.* She shivered slightly as she remembered how she used to wake up in the middle of the night, trembling with anxiety over whether to stay in Missouri where her kids could be close

> *"I am 70 now and God has taken care of every need I have ever had. Every one!"—Edith*

∽

to their dad or to move to Ohio where her family and support were. One night when sleep wouldn't come she clutched her covers with white-rimmed knuckles, as she frantically reviewed all the different scenarios she could imagine for herself and her children. None of them seemed like very good options. "What should I do, Lord?" she called out in the darkness. "I don't want to take the children away from their father, but I can't live like this either."

A few weeks later sitting in church during a prayer meeting, she received her answer. Soothing organ music played as everything around Edith slowly faded into the background. She couldn't hear the music or anything else around her. There was no sound as a white light and a powerful presence appeared in front of her. She clearly heard two words: *BE STILL*.

It was a transforming moment for Edith. She stopped worrying and decided she would go to Ohio that summer to see if she could find a house. She gave herself a deadline of August first. If she found a house by then, she would move with her kids; if not, she would stay. She felt at peace.

That summer on exactly August first, Edith found a home (which she still lives in today, nearly 40 years later).

When friends helping her move arrived at Edith's Missouri apartment on a scorching morning in August, she had all their life possessions meticulously organized. Brown boxes were packed and labeled for each room. Their white suitcases for the road trip were set aside, along with a carefully mapped route to guide them to their new home. She had even figured out each stop they would make between their apartment building in Missouri and their new doorstep in Ohio.

> *"God promised me He would walk with me the whole way. He has been good on His promise."*
> —*Edith*

She felt in complete control until friends loaded her family room couch into the moving truck. As she stood in the middle of the empty room, she brokenly wept. "I'm sorry," she stammered to one friend. "This furniture, this apartment, is all so symbolic to me. It is where we set up our home together."

After a long, hard cry, Edith said a final good-bye to her Missouri home and seat-belted her kids into their car for the road trip. As she drove across the state, she thought about how she would set up their new home. Because finances were very tight she would have to be creative to provide a warm, secure home for her children. She was determined to make things simple but special.

During their first year in Ohio Edith used her thrifty mind-set and instituted Friday Family Night. Every Friday after school the children raced into the house and went straight to the kitchen drawer for the local take-out restaurant menu. After they scoured the menu and selected their meals, Edith phoned in their order with three sets of ears listening to make sure she got it right. Once the order was placed, the kids sat watching out the window, anticipating the magical delivery of their dinners. Even Samson, their cat, got excited when the yellow-and-white delivery truck pulled up. Eating their dinners on TV trays, they always watched the latest episode of their favorite television show and then played games afterward. It was an inexpensive, yet big treat for the kids.

> *"To hang on to my worries means that I am still trying to be my own savior."—Edith*

Although Friday Family Night proved to be a big hit, the children's favorite night was Banana Split Night, which unfolded quite by accident.

One night while cooking dinner, Edith announced with a beaming smile, "I have a surprise after supper tonight!"

"What is it?" asked the children in unison.

"You'll have to wait and see. Eat your dinner then I'll show you." She walked away from the table, grinning.

While the kids gulped down their dinner, Edith went into the kitchen and made mouth-watering, double-decker, hot-fudge banana splits.

"Ta-dah!" she announced proudly, setting the desserts on the table. The kids dug in greedily but after just a few bites, they began to moan. They were too full from dinner to enjoy them. *Well, the heck with this,* Edith thought, staring at the melting banana splits. *From now on if we have banana splits, they will just have to be our dinner.* After that, Edith served decadent banana splits for dinner a few times each year.

Edith even learned to trust God and not worry when the kids flew to Missouri to visit their father. The next year when she drove away from the airport after bidding her children good-bye, she resolved,

I'm not going to drive myself insane this time. Paying the parking attendant, she made up her mind to do something productive while the children were gone. To pass the time she did something creative to each of the children's rooms. In Patty's room she put on a fresh coat of paint using her favorite shade of yellow. In the boys' room she made some homemade curtains out of blue-and-tan checked material and put a fresh coat of paint on their chest of drawers.

> *"I knew I could take the pieces that were left and make the very best life for my kids. I could still make a dream out of it."—Edith*

From that trip on it became a tradition. Every time the kids flew out to see their father, Edith got busy and did something fun to their rooms.

Today, Edith's contagious laughter fills the room as she reminisces about Banana Split Night and all the precious memories she has of raising her children. But then, after a good laugh, her brow furrows and her tone becomes serious. "I had to make a choice along the way. I had to decide to allow God to pick up the pieces of my life and remold them into a new life with new dreams for me and my kids."

She pauses and says with a broad smile, "And He did it. He's never let me down."

In Their Footsteps

"Do whatever it takes to enjoy your children. This will help in your nurture, instruction, and discipline of them."
—*Mary, 57*

"Relax about your TO DO list or being super involved outside your home. The time while your children are young passes way too quickly, and the blessings of enjoying your children at every stage are well worth the sacrifices of not having everything in order or extra material possessions."
—*Jane, 65*

"Give your children *time* not *things.*"
—*Diane, 55*

"Don't only enjoy your children but also make sure they know you enjoy them."
—*Gail, 58*

Annette

It's hard to trust God with our children, especially when things don't go as we planned. This is a story of a mom who, after a long, hard journey, finally surrendered her rebellious son to God, saying, "Lord, I trust You. He is Yours and I trust You completely."

Annette heard the back door open and the familiar footsteps of her 14-year-old son, Billy, as he shuffled into the kitchen. She rinsed the last dish and turned her head toward him. "Hey," she smiled.

Billy collapsed onto a kitchen chair without a word. He bent over and began taking off his tennis shoes. Annette watched, wondering about his abnormal movements. He seemed awkward and unsteady. She wiped her hands on a dishtowel and walked over to him.

"Are you all right?" she asked, holding his shoulders and gently shaking him. Not looking up, he swayed to one side. "Billy!" she shook him a little harder. Annette, a nurse, thought he might be having a seizure.

She crouched down to see his face. She quickly withdrew. He reeked of alcohol. She put her fingers under his chin and lifted it up to look into his glazed, bloodshot eyes.

"Don!" she shrieked to her husband. The urgency in her voice brought Don sprinting into the kitchen. "He's drunk!" Annette said glaring at Billy in disbelief.

Together, Don and Annette carried Billy upstairs for a cold shower. As Don helped Billy get undressed, Annette ran into their bedroom and called the hospital where she worked. "How do you tell if someone has alcohol poisoning?" she blurted out to a co-worker.

Annette hung up the phone after learning about all the symptoms she needed to look for. When Don came into the room and told her Billy had thrown up, she said, "Oh thank God," and dropped onto the bed.

Don looked at her, puzzled.

She pointed to the phone. "I just called the hospital and asked how we would know if he has alcohol poisoning. Throwing up is a good sign that he won't get it."

Don and Annette looked blankly at each other for a moment, then anger struck Annette like an electric volt.

"What was he thinking?" She looked at Don with blazing eyes then stood up and started pacing around the room.

Don stared out the window and shook his head. "I don't know."

The next day Annette knew Billy felt awful—his face was white as flour, and he had gotten out of bed only to go to the bathroom. Annette and Don relished his discomfort, hoping that this experience would teach him never to do it again.

Several weeks later, Annette went into Billy's room to put away his laundry. Opening the sock drawer, she noticed a small plastic bag stuffed underneath some socks at the back of the drawer. She removed the bag and opened it. Inside she found marijuana and smoking paraphernalia. Annette sank onto the bed, her eyes frozen on the little bag in her hands. She tried to wrap her mind around what this bag meant. Her heart pounded. And then her maternal instinct screamed, *No!* She shuddered and looked around his room. *Is there more?* The thought jolted her off the bed. In a frenzy she rummaged through his room.

She didn't find anything else. But what she held in her hands was enough.

That night, Don and Annette sat down to talk with Billy. Annette set the bag on the table between them. "What's this?" Don asked.

Billy shrugged. "I dunno. It's not my stuff. I'm just keeping it for a friend," he lied while maintaining an innocent expression.

Over the next several years Annette's life unraveled as Billy's troubled behavior grew worse. He skipped school, dropped off the track team, and disobeyed curfew. When they grounded him, he sneaked out his bedroom window.

Billy's bad choices and worse behavior crushed Annette. She felt she had failed miserably as a mother. Every night when she tried to fall asleep, torturous questions bombarded her: *How did this happen? What did I do wrong?*

Because she couldn't answer most of the questions that plagued her, she decided to at least try to fix the problem. She immersed herself in finding every possible resource she thought could help Billy turn his life around. She requested a professional assessment from his school. She had him tested for learning disabilities. She had him undergo a psychiatric evaluation. She arranged for him to have counseling sessions at school as well as individual therapy and family therapy.

Nothing helped.

Nothing changed.

After months of fruitless and exhausting effort, Annette came to the end of the available options. She woke early one morning, despair whispering in her ear. *Can you really go on like this? Can you even make it through one more morning?*

No, she thought, *I can't.*

Tears burned in her eyes and she felt a physical weight pressing upon her heart. Sick in body and spirit she choked on her prayer. *Please, Lord, where did I go wrong? I'm his mother. I'm responsible for all this.*

Every day she spent countless hours racking her brain trying to figure out what major mistake she had made. She had a good marriage, went to church and loved God, was involved in her children's lives, wasn't a stern disciplinarian but not a pushover either. What happened?

Annette met with a counselor who helped her process her emotions and grief. Through many hours of counseling Annette began to accept that she wasn't to blame for her son's choices. She realized that there is no assurance that a child raised in a loving, godly home will grow up to make sound, godly choices. Instead, Billy's addictive personality, combined with the influence of drug-involved friends, caused him to make the choices he did.

It took time for Annette to process these thoughts. Meanwhile, Billy's behavior continued to plummet. His drug habits became more serious as he progressed from alcohol and marijuana to harder drugs like cocaine and amphetamines. He dropped out of school and started getting picked up by the police. Some nights, he simply did not come home.

One time, Billy didn't come home for three days. Annette called the police, his friends, anyone she could think of who might help her find him. *I can't live like this, Lord!* she screamed in her mind after making a dozen phone calls. *I have two other children to take care of, a husband, and a job.* Just then the screen door opened and Billy sauntered in. "Hey, Mom," he said casually.

"Where have you been?" demanded Annette, white hot with rage.

"Mom, stop worrying. I was just with friends." He kissed her cheek and bounded up the stairs.

Speechless, Annette stared after him. *We have no control. What should we do? Kick him out of the house?* Her throat tightened. *But he's only 16. Where would he go?* It hurt too much to think about.

At 17, after several serious arrests, Billy was committed to a detention center for hard-core juvenile offenders. After serving time for eight months, he was placed in a group home.

Annette and Don had to make a tough choice about where he would live after his release. It took a long time and much prayer before they came to their difficult decision. He had disobeyed the rules of their house for too long. Their hearts broke when they told him, "We love you very much—but you can't live at home anymore."

With Billy out of the house, life felt a little more normal for Annette as she tended to her other children. Yet her heart never stopped agonizing a single minute over her oldest son.

Out on his own, Billy continued to spiral downward. One drug addiction led to another. In time, he became a heroin addict.

One afternoon he dropped by the house for a visit. Annette stared at her emaciated, addicted son sitting across the kitchen table. She swallowed hard trying to contain her emotions. He couldn't have weighed more than 95 pounds and he looked like a street person. His long, stringy hair hung down over his dirty, unshaven face.

Annette looked into her son's distant eyes. *The heroin is going to kill him,* she thought. *Please, God, don't let him die.* A lump lodged in her throat as she sat in silence with her son. She and Don had tried everything in their power to help him, but nothing worked.

After that visit Annette didn't hear from Billy for months. One evening when sleep would not come, Annette wept. "We don't know if he's dead or alive," she said to Don.

Weighted down by the same heavy loss in his own heart, Don wrapped his arms around his wife. "I know. But we need to keep praying and hoping."

By the time the Christmas season began, Billy had been gone for nine months. One cold Saturday morning in early December, snow flurries swirled around outside as Annette sat at the kitchen table sipping her coffee and reading the morning paper. Looking out the window she felt festive. She decided it would be a good day to dig out the Christmas decorations and trim the tree. Glancing back at the paper, her eye caught the headline of an article toward the bottom of the page: "Unidentified Young Man Dies of Drug Overdose." Her heart pounded. She looked away, not wanting to read the rest. Taking a deep breath, she forced herself to continue. *The victim appears to be approxi-*

mately 20 years old. . . . Anyone who thinks they can help identify the body, please contact the police. The description of the dead man fit Billy perfectly: thin, approximately 5' 10", brown hair, and blue eyes. Annette's whole body convulsed with fear. She couldn't move or talk. After staring out the window for a long time, she numbly got up, walked upstairs to the bedroom, and handed Don the paper. Tears gushed down her cheeks as she pointed to the article. Don's face turned white as he read.

> *"Sometimes it's a process to learn to let go and totally trust God. The process is so very difficult. But I wouldn't trade the lessons for anything."*
> *—Annette, 51*

They stood in silence for a long moment before Annette found her voice. "You'd better go look at the body." Together they went downstairs. Don picked up his jacket and walked out the front door. Annette stood speechless, watching him go. The entry seemed to grow smaller as the door shut behind him. Her head began to spin. She collapsed into a broken heap on the bottom stair in their front hallway and sobbed.

After several minutes something caught her attention. Turning her head she saw what looked like a pile of broken glass or diamonds heaped up in the corner of their hallway. Her mind felt foggy.

What is that? she wondered in confusion.

Through her tears she noticed how shiny and beautiful the broken pieces looked. As she stared at the pile, she felt God opening her eyes.

Lord, she whispered, *that's me, isn't it? That's my heart. All broken into tiny little pieces. Lord, I surrender this broken heart once and for all. Billy is Yours. Whether he's dead or alive, he is Yours.*

After uttering the prayer, Annette felt a warm blanket of peace envelop her. She closed her eyes, breathing in the peace that had evaded her for so many years. Until that moment, she had felt so burdened, so torn apart by her wayward son. She had carried the burden alone, allowing it to consume every hour of her days. During her prayer of surrender, she felt something physically lifted off her shoulders. The burden wasn't there anymore, or at least she wasn't the one carrying it.

As peace encircled her, the ringing phone broke the silence. Picking up the phone, she heard Don's voice filled with agonizing relief. "Honey, it's not him." His voice faltered. ". . . not him."

Relief swept over Annette, too. She hugged the phone to her chest and started to cry deep, wrenching sobs. *Thank You, Lord.*

Billy remained missing for several more months. But the sense of peace Annette had gained that day lifted her into a new realm of trusting God.

Late one evening Annette answered the phone. Her knees buckled when she heard Billy's voice on the other end of the receiver. "Don," she cried out, "pick up the phone!" With Annette clinging to one receiver and Don another, Billy told his parents that he had been in Virginia and then Florida with his girlfriend. He explained that his girlfriend had told him to get off the heroin or she'd leave him. Now off the hard drug he felt compelled to turn himself into the police for violating his probation. "I can't live like this anymore," he confided to his parents in a defeated voice.

> *"I learned the hard way that God is in control and HE IS TRUSTWORTHY!"—Annette*

◌◌

Billy turned himself in and spent many months in jail. His life came to a turning point during this confinement. Early one morning as he flopped restlessly on his thin mattress, he opened his eyes. The sun peeked brilliantly through his cell window. He lay there quietly staring at the streaming beams of light through the black metal bars. In that moment, the choice became crystal clear to him: He could continue wandering down this road of self-destruction and choose death, or he could take a different road, choosing life.

He chose life and asked Christ to live in his heart.

Although the drug years are behind her, Annette remains grateful for her battle scars because it was in the midst of battle that she found the peace that comes with complete surrender. She discovered how deeply she can trust God with her children and not depend on her own strength and resources. It was when she finally yielded everything to Him, including the life of her beloved son, that she was able to experience the supernatural peace that comes only from God.

> *"It's like you come to the same point as Job when he said, 'Though he slay me, yet will I trust in him.'"*
> *—Annette*

In Their Footsteps

"We need to remind ourselves all the time that God loves our children even more than we do."
—*Betty, 60*

"The relationship you establish with your child when he or she is young is so important for the relationship you have with your child when he or she is a teenager."
—*Roberta, 63*

"We need to surrender our lives, all of our lives, to Christ and trust Him. It is hard to do because we like being in control. But He yearns for our trust. Pray that He can help you gain more trust."
—*Cindy, 55*

"Become a warrior for your child through prayer. God impressed on me very strongly to envision a future for my children regardless of the present circumstances. Every time I prayed for my son I always thanked God for making him a godly man, even when he was a rotten teenager."
—*Andrea, 48*

Mothers Summary

ᥫᩒ

When a little bundle of joy becomes a bigger bundle of energy, many moms toss and turn throughout the night, waking in the morning with dark circles underneath their eyes. Then, when moms breathe a sigh of relief and say good-bye to tantrums, pull-ups, and car seats, they turn the corner, often faster than they could have ever imagined, into the preteen and teen years.

The truth is that raising children is one of the most demanding, frequently overwhelming, responsibilities women face. The myriad of parenting decisions have lasting consequences on children. Handling this awesome task of parenting without guidance from older women who have lived through this phase of life is ridiculous! Even though bookstores are filled with wonderful parenting resources, nothing can replace the firsthand knowledge of an older woman who is willing to honestly and openly discuss her successes and failures as a mom.

The women in this chapter all learned to trust God with their children because His love for their children exceeded even their own. Barbara faced blindness and was physically unable to do what she thought a mother should do. Instead of focusing on what she wasn't able to do, she learned to enjoy the moment with her small children. Eileen learned to relax and trust God with her kids, especially when she realized she wasn't the one in control. Annette did everything she could think of to raise her children well, but her son made a string of really bad choices. As a result Annette had to surrender the hope that she could fix him and trust God with his life. Edith allowed God to rebuild her broken dreams for her children—dreams shattered because of circumstances beyond her control. All of these women offer examples of

inspiration to stressed-out moms as they tackle the difficult job of raising their precious children. Following their examples can help any anxious mother sleep peacefully through the night.

What is your greatest fear about raising children?

In what areas are you trying to remain in control of your children
and not allowing God to take control?

What three character traits do you feel are the most important ones
for you to build in your children? How are you modeling these traits?

List three mothers who are good role models for you. What qualities do you admire about them?

Do you trust God with your children's lives? How do you? How
don't you?

What three simple things can you do for your children this week to
communicate your love and care for them? (Ideas: Place a note of
encouragement in their lunch box. Make heart-shaped pancakes. Put a
chocolate kiss on their pillow. . . .)

Suggestions:

1. Spend time each day, even if it's for only five minutes, sitting
   with your kids and doing something silly, like playing slapjack or
   tic-tac-toe, or coloring a picture.

2. Commit time every day to pray for your children. Make your
   prayers very specific. Maybe find another mom you can pray and
   share confidential prayer requests with.

3. Know who your kids are out with, where they are, and what they
   are doing. If you suspect anything is wrong, don't ignore it or tell
   yourself you are just overreacting. Look into it.

4. Make certain you still have time together as a family. Set aside
   one day as family day and take time to do fun things together,
   eat together, and talk together.

chapter four

where women walked . . .

through living single

Sally

*After a series of relationships, 41-year-old Sally was single.
Instead of fighting her "aloneness," Sally allowed God to
become the man in her life—a choice that ultimately
transformed her into the woman He had created her to be.*

Inside her cottage home Sally sat Indian-style on the chenille love seat
clutching her favorite fleece blanket. She looked out the window and
stared blankly at the early morning drizzle. It seemed to be picking up
and turning into a full-fledged spring rain.

"Well, here we are," she spoke in a heavy voice to Ted, her golden
retriever. He stretched lazily on the wood floor next to her, answering
her with silence. Sally hated the silence. She hated being alone. For the
past 15 years there had been one man or another in her life. As she
looked out the window at the dreary day, her mood matched the
weather. The silence began to hum in her ears and a wave of fear swept
through her. *I'm not good at being alone,* she thought, uncrossing her legs
and rolling onto her side. She hugged her knees to her chest, curling up
into a ball. *Maybe I should get up and do something,* she told herself. But
she didn't move. She contemplated calling her best friend, Lisa, but
quickly dismissed the thought. *Not on Lisa's anniversary weekend.*

Her thoughts then drifted to Brendan, her 10-year-old son who was at a friend's house for a sleepover. *I hope he's having fun. Maybe I should call and remind him to wear his helmet if he rides his bike.* Still she lay there numbly watching the rain through the wet windowpane.

She closed her eyes and let visions of Brendan's dad play in her mind. Dan loved to have fun and was always the life of the party. When they got married that is what they did well together—have fun. They ran a small restaurant and partied a lot. Sally played her role as the "fun" wife well. She even overlooked Dan's chronic drinking because she reasoned it was just his way of having fun. The fun crumbled into pieces when Dan died after a short, vicious battle with colon cancer. They had been married seven years and Dan's death left Sally a widowed, single mom of then four-year-old Brendan.

Sally smiled sadly at the memory. *What would have happened if Dan had lived?* she wondered as Ted nudged her for a rub. Sally massaged his ears then grimaced as she thought about her next marriage.

Within a year after Dan's death Sally married a neighbor. *I was the classic single mom who got married for all the wrong reasons,* thought Sally. *Rick seemed like such a responsible guy and he was so good with his own two sons. I just thought . . .* Sally shuddered under her blanket at the foolishness of her decision. Marriage to Rick proved to be a disaster. He treated Brendan poorly and Sally even worse. After four verbally abusive years, Sally called it quits and divorced him.

After Rick came Jeff. Tears welled up in her eyes as Sally thought about their recent breakup. *How can I be so glad something didn't work out but hurt so much at the same time?* she pondered as her heart sank. Picturing Jeff in her mind, she smiled weakly. She had felt so free riding on the back of his motorcycle pretending she didn't have a care in the world. Swept up by the thrill of the moment Sally quickly became engaged to Jeff right after she divorced Rick. But the romance disintegrated when she found out he was seeing another woman.

The tears brimming in her eyes spilled onto her cheeks. Combing her fingers through Ted's thick fur coat, she let out a loud sigh laced with regret. As she inventoried her broken relationships, a thought suddenly blew through her like a bone-chilling wind. *I acted very differently with each one of these men.* She sat straight up on the love seat, knocking the fleece blanket onto Ted. *There is a distinct pattern here*, she thought as another bolt of alarming realization struck her: *I became whatever the guy wanted me to be.*

"Yuck," Sally said, disturbed with herself. She stood and walked over to the window. *I'm a chameleon,* she thought, swallowing hard. She felt frightened. Sally's tears now matched the steady stream of rain outside as she asked herself, "Who am I?"

> *"God wanted me as a single person because He had a plan for my life and I kept trying to implement my own plan for my life not His."*—Sally, 53

She looked out the window for a long moment and then slowly walked over to the coffee table where she kept her Bible. Picking it up, she began to pray. *Now that You have me alone, Lord, maybe it's time that I found out who I am.*

She sat back down and closed her eyes. The pitter-patter of the rain softly played outside and calmness filled her. In the quietness of her spirit she felt the Lord tenderly whisper her name. *Yes, Sally. It's time to find out who I created you to be.*

Over the next seven years, Sally enjoyed the exciting journey of discovering precisely that. She had been what others wanted her to be for so long that it took time to uncover her real interests and gifts.

First, she got involved with her church drama team as an outlet for her lifelong love of acting. Sally also began volunteering at a nearby retirement home. Each week, she and Ted would visit elderly people. They brightened the residents' day just by the friendly wag of Ted's tail and Sally's winsome smile.

Sally joined a women's Bible study group and became a board member of a local Christian Women's Club. Her priorities changed for

the first time in her life. Instead of trying to please a man, she wanted
to please God.

As a single person, Sally also found many small ways in day-to-day
life in which she could allow God to be the man of her house. She came
to Him with financial problems, parenting problems, and even little
logistical household nuisances that she formerly believed she needed a
man for.

One day as Sally tried to fix her broken dishwasher, she cried out
in utter frustration. "Lord! I don't know what I'm doing here! I need
help!" All of a sudden a picture of some obscure tool flashed through
her mind. *I think I have seen that tool out in the garage*, she thought. *But
I don't have a clue what to do with it.*
She marched out to the garage and
dug around in the tool chest. "What
do you know? There it is!" she said
with surprise as she snatched the
tool. Looking up, she held the tool
in her hand. "But now what do I do
with it?" she asked. Sally went back to the kitchen, tool in hand, and
before she knew it, she had fixed the dishwasher. "What do you know?
We did it, God!" she laughed.

> *"God doesn't just want
> me part-time. He wants
> me full-time."*
> —*Sally*
>
> ᏊᎧ

God also directed her during this time in her life to work on broken relationships. In particular, He prepared her heart to let go of a lifelong anger she held against her mother. The seeds of bitterness had
been planted in Sally's childhood when, at a young age, she took care
of her alcoholic mother. Even after her mother stopped drinking, the
root of resentment was so firmly planted that Sally couldn't see past it.
But as she drew closer to God, the decades of bitterness and resentment
melted away in her heart.

Before her mom died, Sally spent many hours at her bedside,
brushing her hair, stroking her arm, and gently ministering to her. The
woman who ravaged her childhood became precious to Sally. *This is all
You, Lord,* Sally prayed while driving to see her mom at the nursing

home one afternoon. *Because I know I would've been too hardened and preoccupied with my life to have ever done this on my own.*

While Sally felt a new closeness and intimacy with the Lord, she still had moments where being single in a couple-oriented world felt very hard. Every week at least one person asked her the question "Do you ever think about being married again?"

"Of course I do. I've always loved men!" Sally laughed at her joke every time.

> *"He was so faithful to me, you would never believe it. The everyday deal-with-it issues that I might have normally taken to a husband, I brought to God. And He took care of them."—Sally*

Although her response appeared lighthearted, deep down she did yearn for a life partner. Like everything else, she talked it over with God. "You know my heart, Lord. I desire a husband, someone I can walk through life with."

Sally even got out her pen and paper and wrote out the qualities she wanted in a husband. She had written lists in the past, but this one was different. Now her first priority was a godly man.

During her time as a single person, another difference had evolved inside her—she no longer felt anxious about being alone. She knew God in a different way. She trusted Him and His plans for her life. Not wanting to interrupt God's sovereignty in her life, she learned to cling to Jeremiah 29:11, which says: "*'For I know the plans I have for you,' declares the* LORD, *'plans to prosper you and not to harm you, plans to give you hope and a future.'*"

Trusting His plan transformed Sally's emotional life. On Sunday mornings she could walk into church with God's promise tucked in her heart and not feel envious or distressed as she looked around at all the happily married couples.

Today, Sally sits curled up on the same chenille love seat that once occupied her cottage home. But now the love seat is perched in front of a picturesque window in a quaint Santa Fe–style house that she shares with her husband, George. Two years ago, in God's perfect timing, Sally met George at church.

As much as Sally cherishes her new husband and their God-centered marriage, she also treasures her many years as a single person. "If I had gotten into another relationship that God didn't want for me, I would have missed all those precious years with Him as the only man in my life." They were years filled with discovering who she was, a total dependence on God, and the healing touch of His tender hand. It was also the time in Sally's life in which she shifted priorities from her passion for a man to an intimate relationship with God.

"I wouldn't trade those years for anything," says Sally, "because now I am totally myself. I am the woman God made me to be, not some weak, color-changing chameleon. And it wouldn't have happened without His giving me time out—alone with Him."

In Their Footsteps

"My relationship with the Lord changed when I became single. He became everything to me. Reliance, trust, and my future I put in His hands. My faith has increased."

—Ihla, 65, who was widowed after
32 years of marriage

"Learn to be comfortable with yourself. Learn to like yourself as a single person. You don't need another person to make you whole."

—Gail, 59

"I was widowed one and a half years ago. In this new season I am searching out other widows and singles to teach me from their learned wisdom."

—Helen, 63, who also says she has become
involved in different ministries to keep
herself from feeling lonely

"As women, many times we want to put a bandage over our hurts. But our wounds need air to heal. Like loneliness, we often take a man and try to put him over that loneliness, and that's not what will heal it. A man is not guaranteed to be a good Band-Aid. I've seen a lot of bad Band-Aids out there. Being alone makes us see who we really are and brings out some wonderful qualities in our lives."

—Pat, 55, a widow for 11 years

Jody

As a single mom with four children and little money, Jody relied on God for her every need. As she fervently prayed to Him, He faithfully provided in unexpected ways.

"No knocking on the door please," Jody instructed her four children as she entered the quiet refuge of her bathroom. "Just play quietly and be good for a few minutes." The bathroom was the only room these days where she could find time alone to pray. Jody closed the bathroom door, leaned her weary body against the cold tile wall, and prayed, "God, give me strength to do the things I need to do and the wisdom to do them. . . ."

A few minutes later she heard little voices whispering and a shuffling of paper. She opened her eyes and saw a scroll of white paper slowly appear underneath the closed door. She reached for it and unrolled it. Written in Dan's seven-year-old handwriting, it read, "Deer mommy kan u get us sum mlk and becky needz togo potte." She smiled at her children's ingenuity, opened the door, and answered their pleas for help.

Life was not easy as a single mother of four. The responsibility of providing for all of their physical, emotional, and spiritual needs at times felt overwhelming. Having nowhere to turn but to God, she prayed every little chance she had and discovered what an awesome, loving God can do when you turn to Him for help.

Jody and her children lived in a small apartment. The three boys shared one room and she and her daughter shared the other. As the children grew, the small space began to feel very crowded. She began praying that God would provide a house for her to raise her children in. But as a single mom working part-time as a labor and delivery nurse, Jody knew that buying a house was a big request. Even the realtors told her it was inconceivable. Undaunted by their pessimism, Jody prayed and started searching for a home.

"Come on, kids!" Jody hollered. "Jump in the car. Let's drive around and look at houses." The kids climbed into the old station wagon and Jody drove around neighborhoods she thought might be a possibility.

"Mom, how about that one?" Dan said, pointing to a house with a For Sale sign in the front yard.

"Let's take a look." Jody parked the car and all five of them piled out and ran around the vacant house peeking in the windows. *This house is painted the ugliest color of green I think I've ever seen!* she thought with a grimace on her face.

"This is like a mansion!" exclaimed Cameron. "It has three bed-rooms!" Then the children each shared what they loved about the home. For all of them, the park that sat on the north side of the house offered the biggest yard any of them could have imagined.

Jody restrained her excitement. *I probably couldn't afford this house anyway, but it never hurts to pray*, she thought. She gathered her flock of kids around her on the front porch and prayed, "God, this house is perfect. It's big and has such a beautiful park next door, giving the kids room to run. If it's Your will, make it happen. Love You! In Jesus' name we pray, amen." They scampered back to the car and drove away.

That night, while eating supper, Jody and the kids talked excitedly about the possibility of buying the house.

"I don't know if this is the house God has planned for us. But if it is, I noticed it doesn't have a refrigerator. We will need to save some money to buy one," Jody explained to them.

"That's okay, Mom," answered Dan. "We can save up the money."

"Yeah, but we will have to make some sacrifices. One thing we can do to save some money is to start shutting off the lights we aren't using," Jody said.

Suddenly, the phone rang. It was her pastor.

"Jody," he said, "you don't need a refrigerator do you?"

Jody almost dropped the phone. "Pastor Bob, you're not going to believe this. We looked at a house today. It is perfect for us. The only thing missing is a refrigerator!"

"Well, someone donated one to the church today, and I just thought you might need it."

"We'll take it!"

Jody took this as a sign from God that if He gave them the refrigerator, then He would somehow provide that house. So the next day she called the realtor and toured the house. Jody couldn't believe it when the realtor told her the price of the house. "That's in my price range," she said with a giant grin.

A few months later, Jody and her kids moved into the house and painted it a beautiful bright green. They have lived in it ever since.

Times were tight, and often Jody lived from paycheck to paycheck, depending on God to fill the in-betweens. For example, one time they were almost out of groceries and Jody wasn't expecting a paycheck for another week. On top of that, her daughter, Becky, had a persistent hankering for a banana. Knowing her mom couldn't buy any until the next week, Becky prayed for some bananas without telling her mom.

Later that same day a neighbor walked in with some extra fruit she had bought. Becky jumped down the stairs yelling excitedly, "Oh good, the bananas are here!"

"What bananas?" Jody asked, thinking Becky must have asked the neighbor for some.

"The bananas I prayed for," Becky announced, pointing at the gift in the neighbor's hands.

Today, Jody and Becky still ask each other, "Where is your banana faith?" in moments when they need a reminder of what God can do with the faith of a child.

Sometimes God provided the desires of her children's hearts when they didn't even pray for them. For example, one Christmas the four children talked about what they would want for gifts if they had money. Her 11-year-old son, Dan, dreamed of owning a stereo, while nine-year-old Cameron wanted a record player. Becky, seven, wanted a suitcase, and Shannon, five, imagined a race car set. God knew Jody's kids weren't greedy. They were just dreaming. But once again God provided.

Shortly before Christmas, a nurse Jody worked with mentioned she was getting her daughter a new stereo and wondered if Jody wanted the old one. A few days later, another nurse told Jody she had cleaned out her grown children's stuff stored in her garage and asked if Jody wanted any of it. One item was a record player. Then, just a few days before Christmas, another nurse handed Jody two things: a red-and-white child's suitcase and an electric race car set. God provided each item the children had dreamed of.

Not only did God provide for Jody's and her children's physical needs and desires but He also pro-

> *"The best advice my mom ever gave me was to take time for myself and not to feel guilty about it. If you re-energize, you'll be a better parent. I went away every few months for a personal weekend retreat."—Jody, 50*

∽

vided wisdom to Jody as she sought His guidance. Jody constantly prayed to God for help as she tried to raise her children alone. One time, God unexpectedly answered this prayer through her son Dan. As she stood at the kitchen counter chopping vegetables for dinner, he told her the adventures of his day. Jody was concentrating on feeding the younger children and finishing her chores for the day. "Uh-huh, yeah," Jody responded, nodding her head once in a while.

Frustrated with her inattention, Dan placed his hands on her face and turned her head toward him. He looked into her eyes, touching the very center of her soul, and said, "Mom, this is a two-eared story." From then on she made an effort to listen to her children with both ears.

As her children grew older, Jody's prayers grew longer and sometimes more desperate. Through the bumpy teenage years, Jody faithfully upheld her children in prayer. She often prayed for wisdom in parenting and found that God faithfully gave her insights for relating with each of them in special ways. For example, one day as Jody prayed for Dan, she felt God gave her the revelation that her oldest son shared his struggles more openly when fishing. So she began to take him fishing more often at a nearby lake. She cherished their time together— hearing him talk as they sat side by side, fishing poles in hand, casting into the lake in hopes of catching a big one.

> *"I am so thankful that whenever I knocked on the Lord's door, which was often, He always answered my cries for help."—Jody*

One night several years after Dan had moved out of the house, Jody heard a knock on her door. She glanced at the clock. *Two in the morning. I wonder who that is?*

She woke a little more to the persistent knocking. *It's probably Dan. He's the only one who would knock on my door at this hour.*

Jody rolled out of bed and opened the door to her son's smiling face.

"Hey, Mom, wanna go fishin'?" her now 21-year-old son asked.

"Sure," Jody answered, laughing before a yawn escaped her mouth. "I'll get my gear."

They drove to a nearby lake, took their fishing poles out of the car, baited their hooks with worms, and started casting their lines into the dark water. Together they sat and enjoyed the sounds of the night, like the occasional splash of the water at their feet and the songs of the bull-frogs that echoed across the lake. Then Dan broke the silence and began sharing the burdens that lay on his heart. He shared his struggles with her while she listened and silently prayed for him. Occasionally, she would offer some motherly encouragement.

Jody listened for nearly an hour when she felt a tug on her line. She set the hook and the rod bent, almost touching the ground.

"Mom, you've got a big one!" Dan exclaimed. Together, they fought and reeled in a 10-pound catfish at 3:30 A.M. Enjoyment mingled with laughter as together, they drove back home, their hearts connecting once again.

Today Jody prays just as much, if not more, than she used to. It's not uncommon for her to wake up during the night and be moved to pray for someone. The pastor of her church even gave her a key so she can go to the sanctuary anytime and stay as long as she wants. God faithfully provides answers to her persistent prayers—not always the answer she expects, but always an answer. "Recently, I read the verses in Luke 12:22-34 about not worrying about what you eat or drink. This made me realize that our God knows our needs before we even know they are a need. But through our fellowship with Him in prayer, He is able to grow and mature us with His wisdom while providing for our basic needs. That empowers us to carry out our mission as a mom," Jody says. Through the years, she's learned that God is a provider. He delights in answering prayer, but even more, He delights in hearts, like Jody's, that turn to Him for every need.

> *"God always listens with both ears, never needs time away, and is available any time."—Jody*

In Their Footsteps

"Trust only in God. He alone is your strength."
—*Anonymous, 64*

"Always have room in your life for the Lord. As circumstances change He is always there for you."
—*Anonymous, divorced after 31 years of marriage*

"Do not feel in the least bit guilty to pick up your personal interest for a short, revitalizing break in your life of service. It will assure you of who you still are and of your personal worth."
—*Anonymous*

"Times were difficult in my home growing up. My father drifted away from the Lord, making all of our lives miserable. But, it was during this time that I learned to trust the Lord. One thing that helped me most during this time was seeing my mother pray. Many times I found her on her knees in the basement, casting her cares on the Lord."
—*Anonymous, 65*

"When I would grow weak from hunger, someone would show up with a hot meal and a hug. I became aware that God provided countless people in countless ways to pray, encourage, physically help, emotionally sustain, and just be there with and for me. He also used His very creation to lighten my heart: a possum who visited daily in the backyard; a beautiful, unique bug on the screen door; a splendid sunset; and the fullest moon overhead as I stepped outside for a breath of air."
—*Peggy, 53, who cared for her dying mother*

"Because I didn't have the support of a husband, I learned to turn to God in everything . . . and He meets every one of my needs."
—*Beth, 60*

Living Single Summary

❧

Being single is not a death sentence. Nor is it wise to view singleness as a temporary state until we get married. There is a full life to be lived when we aren't sitting around waiting for Mr. Right to come along. And often in the process we meet wonderful people.

More and more, women are single—whether divorced, widowed, or never-married. Some women feel neglected and forgotten by the married world. It's painfully true that being single isn't easy in a society that caters to couples and families. Treated as outcasts or as people no one is quite certain what to do with, singles often stumble along, wanting to develop relationships with people. It's tough for singles to find support systems, people to celebrate holidays with, and friends to talk to.

While being single can be tough, with its own unique challenges, it can also be an exciting, fulfilling adventure. Single women seeking God develop the most awesome relationships with Him. He becomes their companion, guide, wise counselor, and best friend.

The women in this chapter are examples of women choosing to accept and enjoy their singleness. They each turned to God and relied on Him as their most intimate companion. After a string of broken relationships, Sally found herself alone with God and discovered who He had created her to be. Jody, a single mom, trusted God as her provider, and He never failed her.

"Don't waste time looking for a man," many women advise. "God will send one if that's His plan. Spend time with the people God has put in your life and grow in your relationship to Him."

How do you feel about yourself as a single person? List your strengths and your weaknesses.

How do you feel about God as your most intimate friend? How can you improve your relationship to Him?

Are there any relationships currently in your life that you can spend time on improving? (Children? Grandchildren? Parents? Friends?) What steps can you take to renew and improve these relationships?

Suggestions:
1. Do something new today.
2. If you're not currently volunteering somewhere, start. Find a ministry position that energizes you and plug in.
3. Find an older single woman you can talk to about your fears and feelings. Spend time together once a month.
4. Go on a date with God.
5. Invite a single person (and her children if she has them) over on a Sunday or a holiday.
6. Visit and make friends with an elderly single woman. Go to museums, art shows, concerts, and the theater together.

chapter five

where women walked . . .

and strengthened their faith

Ihla

*Grace is God's unmerited favor. There is nothing
we do to obtain it, and it is a gift He gives us.
What does this gift of grace look like? Just as gifts come
in all sizes and packages, so does God's grace. Here is a
story of a woman who faced crisis and, throughout her
journey, experienced God's grace in many different ways.*

Bumping down the pothole-infested road with other missionaries in a rickety old Land Rover, Ihla looked out over the African landscape and breathed in the beauty of the lush grassland and rolling hills. She had been a missionary in Uganda with her husband, John, for the past six years and now Africa felt like home.

As she savored the scenery, her minded drifted to the people to whom she had become so attached. These people did not hurry their way through life like Americans. Their culture valued relationships above anything else and they spent all their free time visiting others and taking care of friends in need. The genuine warmth and hospitality of the African villagers had captured Ihla's heart and now there was nowhere else she would rather live.

The truck jerked them toward Kampala, the capital of Uganda, where John would be speaking at a conference. Ihla smiled as she thought about her unconventional life. She had three children in college. She could be quietly enjoying the "empty nest" stage of life in the safety of their comfortable Colorado home. Instead, she sat squished between two men in the front cab of an old truck, lived in a poverty-stricken African village, and had fallen in love with a people who spoke a foreign language.

Ihla continued to get lost in her thoughts while the morning sun crept higher in the sky. The truck was stuffy and the sun blistered down through the windshield as she chatted with the driver and nurse coordinator. They stopped talking when all of a sudden, the truck began careening out of control across the rutted road. Ihla was thrown out the door.

Her mind went black.

When Ihla regained consciousness, she lifted her head and saw the truck on its side 30 feet away. She lay in a ditch, covered in dirt and blood. Someone started screaming. Ihla strained to see where the anguished voice came from. Near the truck she saw one of their missionary staff members, his eyes desperate with pain. Blood squirted from the man's left arm.

> *"Life as a missionary was anything but safe. In fact, a lot of missionaries left the area we were in because of the danger. But we felt we were where God wanted us so we stayed put."—Ihla, 64*
>
> ᏬᏇ

Ihla tried to think through her confusion. *I need to get him my handkerchief so I can tie a tourniquet on his arm and stop the bleeding.* She told herself to move, but her broken body lay immobile. Her eyes were blurry as she craned her neck, trying to find John. *Where is he?* She couldn't see him anywhere. Exhausted, she laid her head back in the ditch and closed her eyes. *Please let him be all right, Lord.*

Her mind continued to spin, trying to sort through the confusion and chaos around her. On one side she could hear someone moaning soft, low cries. From farther away she could hear someone shouting. Confusion reigned.

As she lay unmoving in the dusty ditch, the voices around her slowly faded. A deep, supernatural peace overcame her and she felt like she was in the middle of a silent, peaceful dream. There was a voice in the dream—a comforting, reassuring voice. She felt God's whisper. *Ihla, I am never going to leave you or forsake you. You are going to live.*

From that moment, Ihla felt no fear. She knew that no matter how badly she had been injured, she would live.

Sometime during the next hour, a loud army truck came flying down the narrow dirt road, stopping abruptly when the driver saw the accident site. All eight people who had been in the Land Rover had been seriously injured and lay scattered across the road. Military men gingerly carried all the wounded to the back of their truck and laid them on top of food sacks.

As the men set Ihla down in the truck, she saw her husband lying down in the truck bed. A wave of relief swept over her at the sight of him. He had his eyes closed and he looked peaceful. Ihla drifted into unconsciousness as the truck began making the rugged, two-hour journey to the nearest medical facility. The first hospital they reached did not have any drugs or X-ray equipment, so the military truck continued on for another two hours until it reached a missionary hospital.

When they arrived at a sparsely equipped Catholic hospital, medical workers carried Ihla to a bed, and a doctor examined her. After a few minutes, he turned to the nurses working with him and spoke in a hushed voice. "She'll never survive. Too many injuries and broken bones." He shook his head. "Her only chance would be if we could airlift her to the surgical hospital in Nairobi." The nurses' faces looked dismal. They all knew that was impossible because the insecure political environment in Africa had crippled all air transportation.

That afternoon, as Ihla lay in the missionary hospital with an IV dripping pain medication into her arm, an African village woman visiting her daughter at the hospital recognized Ihla. She knew John and

Ihla were devoted missionaries. When she found out what had happened to them, she immediately began spreading the word to Christians in nearby villages that Ihla needed help. Men and women, most of whom Ihla had never met, walked that evening from villages within a 70-mile radius to gather and pray together in the hospital compound. They spent the whole night in a prayer vigil, asking God to help their sister in Christ.

God's grace became evident at sunrise the next morning. Missionary co-workers had contacted the U.S. embassy, explaining Ihla's desperate plight. After numerous phone calls between high-ranking U.S. and African officials, Mission Aviation Fellowship was miraculously granted special permission to conduct a rescue flight transporting Ihla to a surgical hospital in Nairobi.

As they prepared Ihla to be airlifted, two of her closest missionary friends came to her bedside. The hesitation in their voices and tears in their eyes spoke to her heart. "John?" she asked, her thoughts clouded by the pain medication.

"We're so sorry, Ihla. The doctors said he didn't suffer. After the accident, he never regained consciousness."

The next day, just as Ihla was airlifted out in a tiny plane, the funeral for her husband began at a nearby cathedral. More than 1,000 people attended.

Ihla stayed in Nairobi at a surgical hospital for five weeks recovering from her injuries and surgeries. Every day of her hospital stay, a faithful missionary woman, Deb, visited her. During her first visit Deb sat for a long time by Ihla's bed without a word. Ihla felt the comfort of her presence and drifted in and out of sleep. Before leaving, Deb tenderly picked up Ihla's bruised hands. Looking into Ihla's eyes, she spoke with deep compassion. "Ihla, if God's grace isn't good enough for the big things, it's not good for anything." And Deb knew what she was talking about. Just three months earlier, she had lost her two sons and husband in a terrible car accident also in Africa.

Ihla let the words seep into her heart. *God's grace,* she thought wearily. All at once 2 Corinthians 12:9 seared her mind. She opened her eyes and whispered the words from the verse: *My grace is sufficient for you.* She had always loved that verse. Over and over she repeated the verse in her mind. Before she fell back to sleep, her lips softly murmured, "Those words are for me—aren't they, Lord? Your grace is sufficient for me." She drifted into a peaceful sleep.

Finally, Ihla was flown to the United States, where she spent many months in rehabilitation learning to walk again. One afternoon, at the beginning of Ihla's rehabilitation journey, her orthopedic surgeon walked into the patient room where Ihla waited. His steel blue eyes looked at Ihla as he spoke. "You will have time to grieve, Ihla, but now you need to spend your time and attention on getting better physically. If you don't, then you will find yourself suffering not only grief but also the depression that comes from physical debilitation." Touching her shoulder, he encouraged her, "Put your energy into physically healing right now."

Ihla listened to his words and for the next several months, she spent six grueling hours a day training her legs to move fluidly again. During this recovery time she stayed with family. One night she felt particu-

> *"One doctor told me that according to the stress chart, I should be off the chart because I had lost everything—a husband, a home, a way of life. But I never felt panicked. I felt His presence."—Ihla*

ᕫᕫ

larly exhausted and excused herself to bed early. After she turned out the lights and crawled under her covers, she heard her loved ones speaking in soft tones. "What is she going to do now? Is she going back to Africa? Where will she live?" They fretted back and forth for quite some time. Ihla closed her eyes and rolled over onto her side, tuning out their voices. *You've given me such grace, Lord, that I'm not worried about tomorrow,* she thought and then fell fast asleep.

After Ihla learned to walk again, she returned to Africa to grieve with the people of her village. Sticking with their cultural traditions,

Ihla hosted a feast for hundreds of villagers after a memorial service was held. Joyful music rang out into the air as people danced and ate. They celebrated Ihla's recovery and felt fulfillment in having had the opportunity to grieve alongside her.

After saying many heart-wrenching good-byes to her African friends, she flew back to the United States where she traveled with different relatives for the next year. Finally, two and a half years after John died, she settled into her life as a widow and moved back into the house they had shared before their missionary days. She became involved again at their old church and started volunteering at a local hospice.

One Saturday morning she sat attentively in a hospice volunteer training program, listening to the grief counselor talk about the various stages of grief. Suddenly, a hard truth struck her like a bolt of lightning. *I have not truly grieved yet. I have coasted along in the lap of God's grace and haven't faced my losses.* As she drove home that afternoon, a haze settled over her and she knew it was time to grieve.

The security that enveloped her so warmly during the previous two years molted, and a dark, lonely tunnel consumed her. A few weeks after the hospice training Ihla sat alone in her house and couldn't move. She lay on the living room couch as the walls of the empty house rang in her ears.

Her future seemed so bleak that she felt dread for tomorrow. She stared at her Bible on the side table, and then turned her head. She couldn't pick it up. She didn't care what it said.

For many months she existed in a fog. She battled hopelessness, self-pity, and depression. Even though the hospice grief trainer had said grief takes time, Ihla thought her despair would never end.

During these months Ihla began reading a book called *Loneliness* that Elisabeth Elliot, a Christian author, had sent Ihla shortly after John died. In the book she provided readers specific things to do to help them journey down the lonesome road of grief. Inside the front cover of the book Elisabeth tucked a note that said, "DO THE NEXT

THING." Although Ihla's grief was all-consuming, she made herself faithfully adhere to Elisabeth's advice, reading the book and doing the "next thing."

Gradually, she began to feel a flicker of hope.

Early one morning she woke up and noticed her heart didn't feel weighted down like it usually did. After making a pot of coffee, she sat in her favorite chair and looked out at the mountains. She glanced down at her clenched fists and slowly opened them so that her palms faced up. In a humble voice she prayed, "My life is Yours, Lord. I let go."

As the darkness of grief lightened, Ihla began to recognize His grace again. This time, it looked different. It wasn't in the form of a warm, comforting peace. It was richer and deeper; life felt different. She found inside herself a deep

> *"I try to live a life of gratefulness and hope, being a blessing while being blessed! I look forward to what God has for me in the future and build on the past using what I have been through and learned. HIS GRACE IS SUFFICIENT!"—Ihla*

appreciation for the simple, everyday gifts from God—like her home, hiking and blue skies, friendships and her church, meaningful conversations, and her volunteer work. She began noticing how much God had given her and not dwelling on what she'd lost.

His grace felt sufficient indeed. It had provided a peace that surpassed all understanding from immediately after the accident throughout her physical healing. It continued to sustain her through the dark tunnel of grief. And now, many years after losing her husband, she lives with a rare ability in life—the ability to revel in the ordinary and see His wonderment all around her.

Ihla feels blessed to have lived through many gifts of His grace.

In Their Footsteps

"God is our Comforter. He wants you to rest in His arms. He walks with us through the dark valleys. Cling to Him in the storms of life."
—*Carole, 70*

"When I face hard things, I try to get alone with God and do something creative. I am a painter so lots of times I'll paint and let Him minister to me while I work my paintbrushes."
—*Theresa, 53*

"Try and memorize God's Word in your heart because it helps you get through the hard times."
—*Dottyanne, 52*

"Hold fast to God. He will never fail you, and He is the only one who truly knows and understands your trials and sufferings."
—*Connie, 71, divorced after 43 years of marriage*

Denise

During his times of suffering, the psalmist David
sought out God first thing in the morning.
"In the morning, O LORD, you hear my voice; in the
morning I lay my requests before you and wait in
expectation" (Psalm 5:3). Like David, Denise also gains
her strength from mornings spent with God.

Denise woke a little after 6:00 A.M. Her mind felt groggy from sleep as she rubbed her eyes. A moment later, she remembered she was leaving on a trip later that morning to visit her daughter and was already packed and ready to go. *Good, I can take my time reading my Bible this morning,* she thought, getting out of bed. She slipped on her robe and headed to the kitchen to make coffee. While the coffee brewed, she read the verse on the calendar for the day: "He must increase and I must decrease." *Yes, Lord,* she prayed. *Help me put You first today in everything I do.*

After she poured herself a cup of coffee, she went back to her bedroom and shut the door. First, she picked up her daily devotional and read the excerpt for the day. *Lord, this reading reminds me of John's favorite truth about You: Jesus Christ is the same yesterday, today, and tomorrow.* She looked over at their black-and-white wedding picture and her heart stung. *Lord, You know I'm not the same every day. My emotions are like a roller coaster some days. Help me cling to and trust in Your everlasting steadfastness.* Picking up her Bible, she began to read in the book of John. She always seemed to gain strength and fortitude when she read the Gospels. Just reading the words Jesus spoke filled her with confidence in Christ. *I need confidence today, Lord,* she prayed as she glanced at their wedding photo again. *I always feel so torn when I travel. Give me peace. Your peace.*

As she stared at the photo, she set her Bible down and picked up the picture. She smiled at how young they both looked. And how happy. She had worn a sophisticated pillbox hat that suited her simple satin dress perfectly. And she thought John looked particularly handsome in a traditional black tuxedo. Leaning her head back on a pillow, Denise closed her eyes as her thoughts drifted back to that magical day.

It had been a biting cold afternoon in Saskatchewan, Canada. After a traditional wedding ceremony, they held a reception at a lovely Victorian hotel. Family and friends swarmed the newly married couple and Denise felt giddy with excitement. Gazing around the room, she clasped John's hand, interweaving her fingers with his. The old hotel had an intimate ambiance with its crystal chandeliers, regal curtains, and velvety tapestries. *It's perfect,* she thought dreamily. *Just how I've always pictured it would be.*

Now, nearly 40 years later, she opened her eyes and stared at the photo. A tear trickled down her cheek. *I would never have dreamed it would turn out like this, Lord. Help me cling to the hope in Your Word. The hope in You.*

With a bittersweet smile, she got up and zipped closed her dark brown suitcase that lay on the floor next to her bed. Her emotions continued to jostle back and forth. She couldn't wait to see her daughter, Jill, who lived thousands of miles away in Colorado. At the same time it was hard to leave. Stricken by guilt, she stood immobilized for a long moment. She made herself repeat what she had just been reminded of in her quiet time. *Even when life and circumstances change—Jesus Christ doesn't.* Strengthened by this truth, she broke her gaze from the photo and looked at her watch. She needed to get going if she wanted to catch her plane.

After taking a shower, she got dressed and lugged her suitcase down the hall. She stopped in front of the door to their family room. John sat in his usual position, slumped over in the tweed recliner with his eyes closed. She flinched inwardly. She knew how much he had loved to travel. He would have been so excited about this trip. She walked over to him and gently put her hand on his shoulder. "Jiggs," she spoke in a loving, soft voice, "I'm leaving this morning to visit Jill. How 'bout a kiss before I go?" Like a newborn trying to steady his neck, John strained to look up at her. She bent down and kissed his lips. He lifted his stiff arms up slightly in an attempt to hug his wife. Denise fought tears as she embraced him. "I'll miss you," she whispered into his ear, her voice full of emotion.

Helen, the day nurse, walked into the room while Denise was still embracing John. "Good morning, Mrs. Heyhoe," she chirped with a cheerful smile.

Denise felt so relieved at the sight of Helen. For so many years, it had been such a burden for her to care for John all by herself. But now Helen and a few other nurses made her life a little less difficult.

"I've already given Mr. Heyhoe his shower and fed him breakfast." Helen looked at Denise with compassion in her eyes.

"How'd he eat?"

"He did good, Mrs. Heyhoe. A cup of yogurt and a half cup of the mashed bananas."

Looking back at her husband, Denise shook her head. It still amazed her that his once strong 6' 3", 215-pound body could be so shriveled and frail. His atrophied muscles had been rendered completely useless by the cruel Parkinson's disease, making even the simplest of tasks, like feeding himself, impossible.

Focusing her attention back to Helen, Denise began reviewing explicit care instructions. "If you have any problems at all, please call me. And I'll check in every day."

Driving to the airport, she felt terrible. It was just so hard. All of it. Leaving him. Living with him. Missing him. Tears welled up again as she thought about the man he used to be. So full of life. So kind and gentle. So in charge. So romantic. *Oh, John, I wish you were going to visit Jill with me.*

After checking her luggage, Denise dropped into a chair at her assigned gate. She fought the urge to cancel the trip and drive back to her house. As she watched the planes take off and land, her mind slipped back to when the doctors diagnosed the illness that would rob them of their future. Their lives had been so full and normal. They had three sons and a daughter. John owned and operated the flour mill once run by his father. He loved his work and cherished his family, especially Denise. He always made an effort to buy her little pieces of jewelry or bring her fresh flowers. A deep faith in God resided in the center of their lives. Most nights, John would end his day on his knees praying wholeheartedly to the Lord.

> *"The good times are a blessing and the bad times are a blessing in disguise."—Denise*

⟋⟍

In 1987, the tremors in his hands began, but both John and Denise dismissed it. The tremors grew worse and finally couldn't be ignored. When the doctor told John he had Parkinson's disease, neither one of them had the slightest clue what that meant for their future. In the early stages of the disease, high dosages of medication left John with debilitating side effects; the most disturbing one was dyskinesia, a condition that causes sudden, jarring, involuntary movements.

Denise grimaced thinking about those awful years when John's body would twist and writhe in all different directions, completely out of control. A risky brain surgery had helped the dyskinesia, but the incurable Parkinson's disease continued to rage, aggressively attacking John's nervous system and muscular control.

As the years progressed Denise stood by helplessly and watched John lose all his mental abilities. He slept most of the time and when he was awake, he was shut off from the world in some faraway place where Denise couldn't reach him.

As Denise boarded the plane, she forced her thoughts away from the cruel fallout of Parkinson's disease on their lives. Sitting in her assigned seat, she closed her eyes and pictured her grandchildren. A smile crept onto her face and she dozed off to the loud humming of the jet engines.

Denise walked off the plane into Jill's hearty embrace and enthusiastic "Hi, Mum!" All through waiting for the baggage and driving to Jill's home, they chatted back and forth. When they neared the house, Jill took a deep breath and asked, "How was Dad when you left?"

Denise's blue eyes shimmered with tears. She knew her daughter understood. "Oh you know . . ." Her unsteady voice broke off when she tried to answer.

"He would want you to do this." Jill looked over at her mom. "He wouldn't want you to just stay home and do nothing."

"I know." Her daughter was right. Denise looked out the window as they drove in silence for a few minutes. Then she blurted out, "Your father loved cars."

"He sure did." Jill smiled at her mom.

"One of the hardest things was when they took his driver's license away," Denise continued. "Right before they took it, he bought his first luxury car." She smiled faintly at the memory. "It was a 1990 gold Lincoln."

An easy silence filled the car again. Then Denise spoke, her voice husky. "Sometimes, I would find him standing in the kitchen, looking out the window, just staring at that car."

Both Denise and Jill were crying now. Jill reached over and touched her mom's hand. "Watching him lose all that was probably the hardest part, huh, Mum?"

Denise nodded, taking a tissue from her purse and dabbing her eyes. It felt therapeutic to cry with her daughter. Relief swept through her by just being with someone who understood. By the time they got to Jill's house, they were talking and laughing about the kids and making big plans for her visit.

After shopping outings, school functions, and carting the children to and from their countless activities, Denise boarded her plane home with a renewed spirit. It had felt so good to be in a home bustling with life. It was late into the night when she unlocked the front door at her own house. A surge of loneliness swept over her as she entered the dark hallway. She walked to John's bedroom and peeked in on him. Pulling the sheet up over his chest, she then bent down and kissed his cheek. He lay unresponsive and motionless.

As she walked to their master bedroom, Denise was struck by another bolt of loneliness: *I'm married but I don't share a bed with my husband. I wake up alone and go to bed alone. I'm a widow—only I'm not.*

She crawled into bed feeling a heavy weight settle on her chest. Closing her eyes, she pictured her two grandsons curling up on the floor next to her bed. She missed them already. She rolled over and looked at the empty spot next to her. She craved the warmth of John's body next to her in bed. She pined for his good-night kiss. She longed to talk to him about Jill and the kids. A ripple of despair swept over her as she thought about how they had dreamed about traveling together in their retirement years. As tears slipped down her cheek, spilling onto her pillow, she knew that would never be her life. This was her life—existing year after year with a man who lay downstairs in a dark, handicap-accessible room, closer to death than life.

She awoke in the morning with the sun streaming through her giant picture window. She fought the lonely emotions waiting to overtake her from the night before and slipped out of bed to make coffee before having a quiet time with God. Once the coffee was made, she retreated to her room and picked up her Bible and the daily devotional she had unpacked and placed on the nightstand. Propping up her pillows, she leaned back and began her day like she always did—with

God. *Lord, I'm feeling overwhelmed by this life. I'm empty and weary. Please grant me stamina to face another lonesome day as a caretaker.* She read the Bible for the next half hour. As she read, she felt like she was having an interactive conversation with God. She would read a verse and then pray about it. Sometimes a verse led her to pray for a grandchild, sometimes a verse was confusing and she asked for clarity, and sometimes she claimed a verse for her own life. After reading she set the Bible down and closed her eyes to listen to God. After quietly listening for several minutes she prayed, *Lord, You fill me up. I don't feel empty anymore after spending time in Your Word. Thank You for meeting my needs. Amen.*

As Denise finished her quiet time, a penetrating comfort settled over her, and she felt lighthearted as she got dressed for the day.

Later that morning after tending to John, Denise went out to her blossoming garden. She got on her knees and started pulling weeds and snipping overgrowth. She inhaled deeply, letting the smell of the outdoors fill her. The sun beat down on her back, and a bead of perspiration dribbled down her forehead. Squinting her eyes, she looked up and whispered, "Thank You." She felt revived in her garden and knew He was holding her up again. Through the simple act of working in her garden, she received a daily portion of joy and strength. It wasn't much, but it was enough, and she allowed it to fill her.

Over the years, Denise has found her secret to survival—take it one morning, one day, at a time. "It happens every morning for me. I need to meet God in the morning to make it through my day," she shares. When she is physically weary, she asks for stamina; when she is lonely, she lays her heartache at God's feet asking for comfort; when she is doubtful about the future, she asks for reassurance. Sometimes, He answers her with a specific verse in the Bible. Sometimes, a friend calls with a word of encouragement. Sometimes, laughing with one of her children or grandchildren lifts her up. But she feels His provision for her every day.

"I go only from day to day, and the Lord has supplied me with the health and strength to keep going. My life is really like that poem which talks about how His mercy and strength are new each day."

> God hath not promised skies always blue,
> Flower strewn pathways all our lives through.
> God has not promised sun without rain,
> Joy without sorrow, peace without pain.
>
> God hath not promised we shall not know
> Toil and temptations, trouble and woe.
> He hath not told us we shall not bear
> Many a burden, many a care.
>
> God hath not promised smooth roads and wide,
> Swift easy travel needing no guide,
> Never a mountain rocky and steep,
> Never a river turbid and deep.
>
> But God hath promised strength for the day,
> Rest for the labor, light for the way,
> Grace for the trials, help from above,
> Unfailing kindness, undying love.
> —Annie Johnson Flint, 1919

And Denise has discovered when she comes to Him every morning over a cup of coffee—He is good on His promise.

In Their Footsteps

"Sometimes, when life feels too hard to handle, you just have to live it one day at a time."

> —*Elinor, 84. Many years ago, Elinor was diagnosed with polio. A week later, her husband was diagnosed with the same terrifying disease. She recovered, but was left significantly crippled. At that time they had four small children. Now, after overcoming insurmountable difficulties, she has learned the importance of giving her burdens to God every morning and taking life one day at a time.*

"I try always to remember that God is with me for strength and comfort. He supplies all I need. Not always what I want, but what I need."

> —*Lydia, 81*

"Try and not look inward at all the pain and suffering and hurt you are going through, but look to the Lord for strength to make it through the next second."

> —*Stephanie, 59*

"It is His strength that can carry you through the trial. The battle is His."

> —*Fran, 60*

"My spiritual journey with the Lord has been directly proportional to how much time I spend with Him reading His words—the Bible."

> —*Anonymous*

Janice

Have you ever made a BIG mistake? Janice has.
Several doozies in fact. She could be ashamed and
embarrassed by her mistakes. But instead of sweeping
her past under the rug, Janice has made a choice to be
vulnerable before God and others. She has learned that
God can use her journey—including failures—to build
her character and mold her into His image.

Janice rolled over to snuggle close to her new husband as the early morning sunlight spilled through their bedroom window.

"Mmmmm," she murmured, kissing Darius's back. He rolled over lazily and returned her affection.

"I am so glad we're married. Now we can do this anytime we want," giggled Janice.

"That's why I married you," Darius joked. "So I could have you in my bed."

"You always going to love me?" she asked, nuzzling his neck.

"Of course."

"Take care of me?"

"Yes."

"Protect me?"

"Shhh. Stop talking so much." He had other things on his mind.

Wrapped tightly in his arms, Janice closed her eyes. *We'll always have a happy marriage. We've got everything we need—LOVE.*

In a few years, their baby daughter, Allisa, was born. It seemed the bliss continued—until one night after dinner, Darius slid his leather jacket on and announced, "I'm going out."

"Again?" Janice stopped washing the dishes and looked at him.

"Everyone else my age is still partying. Having fun. Dating around."

"So?" quipped Janice. "You've got a family. What you have is better than all that."

Darius wasn't convinced. "I need to sow my oats, hon. I never got a chance to do that. We got married too young."

"What are you saying? You want to date around? Have you forgotten you HAVE a WIFE and DAUGHTER?" Her mouth hung open in utter disbelief. She stared at him, dumbfounded.

"It's just something I gotta do," he nonchalantly called over his shoulder. He grabbed the keys and strutted out the front door.

Seething, she picked up the phone, punching the numbers as she dialed her best friend. "Alice, who does he think he is?" screamed Janice. "I mean he's acting like this is something he deserves just because we got married young. If he thinks I am sitting by until he gets it all out of his system, he can forget it!"

"How long has he been going out like this?" Alice sounded worried.

"Come to think of it, some time now. I never thought too much of it until tonight. He literally announced what he was doing. The nerve!"

Several months later, divorce papers had been filed. Heartbroken, Janice packed moving boxes in the family room. As little Allisa sat next to her coloring, Janice felt a stab of pain and surge of anger. *Poor little girl is going to be living far away from her daddy—all because he wanted to fool around. I hate that we're getting divorced.* Then came a surge of anger. *How dare he break this family apart!*

After moving, Janice limped along in life without clear direction. One hot, sticky night she was tossing and turning, trying to get comfortable. "It is just too daggone hot in here," she said, getting up to open a window. Poking her head out into the fresh air, she inhaled deeply. It was a clear night and the sky looked like a stadium of twinkling stars. As she stared at the magnificent sky, she thought, *I don't want to go it alone anymore. There is a BIG God out there, and I want Him.* Humbly she cried out to Jesus, whom she had given her life to as a teenager. "Lord, I want to be right with You. I don't want to call the shots in my life anymore. I want You to call the shots. I need You."

> *"We are all a work in progress."—Janice, 56*

Her Christian life started flourishing, and she got involved in ministry work. Absorbed in her work, she had little time to think about men. But then, 11 years after leaving Darius, Prince Charming Number Two walked into Janice's life at a Christian fund-raising event.

"I'm Daniel," he said, holding out his hand, a brilliant smile capturing her attention.

"Nice to meet you," Janice said, hoping her racing heart didn't reveal her instant attraction.

"Your work is incredible," Daniel told her. "It's obvious you believe in this ministry."

"It shows?"

"It shows through your smile, your words, everything."

Janice took a chance, not wanting to let this man go. "Would you like to come to the fellowship meeting with me tonight?"

He accepted without hesitation, and their romance began.

With Daniel around she found herself laughing a lot. "Stop it!" she insisted one night when they were out for dinner. "I mean it! I am going to wet my pants. Quit!" She doubled over, tears running down her cheeks as he told another funny story.

The next morning, she whistled her way into the office.

"What are you whistling about this morning?" queried a co-worker.

"Oh nothing," said Janice, unable to stop smiling.

After happily dating for over a year Janice felt absolutely confident that marrying Daniel was the right thing. When he proposed, she hugged him tightly. But she wanted to be sure. "Daniel this marriage has to be forever."

"I wouldn't have it any other way," he said, scooping her up in his arms with a smile and a kiss.

About a year into the marriage Janice picked up the phone and once again dialed Alice in distress. "Oh Alice, I don't know what I have gotten myself into," she bemoaned. "How could I not have known? How could he have hidden it from me?"

"Will he get help for his drinking?" asked Alice.

Janice shook her head. "He says he will but then he never does."

"Hang in there, honey, and just keep praying for him."

Janice stopped praying when Daniel filed for divorce. "I am sorry, Janice." Daniel wouldn't even look Janice in the eyes. "I just don't want to give up drinking. It's important to me. More important to me than this marriage."

Janice couldn't believe her ears. *Lord!* she screamed inside her head, *how can I have two marriages gone wrong?*

The morning she signed the divorce papers, she felt completely defeated. She drove home, closed the curtains, curled up on the couch, and when the phone rang, she just stared at it. With the ringing in the background, all Janice could hear inside her head was *L-o-s-e-r . . . L-o-s-e-r.*

"I *am* a loser, Lord. I can't get it right. Who am I to do ministry? I can't get my own life right." Feeling beaten by the weight of another broken marriage, Janice decided to close up her heart to men. "I will just serve You, Lord. Forget the rest of this!"

She threw herself completely into ministry. After getting her seminary degree, she began working as an assistant pastor at a large church. Twenty years went by and Janice felt very fulfilled.

Then Prince Charming Number Three pulled up a seat next to her at Bible study. "Hi. My name is Gerry," he smiled.

"I'm Janice. Nice to meet you."

"I am really enjoying this study. I like how the author applies a lot of Scripture to the teaching and it is not all his own thoughts."

> "When we make mistakes we want to sweep them under the rug, pretend they never happened. When we do this God can't use those mistakes to mold us to be more like Him."—Janice

"Me too," said Janice, amazed. "I was just thinking that exact thought this morning while I was doing my lesson."

"Would you like to have coffee sometime?"

"I'm not sure if that is a good idea," hesitated Janice. *I am not doing this again,* she thought. *I don't care how good looking, charming, and CHRISTIAN he is. I'm not doing it.*

But Gerry was persistent, patiently pursuing her each week. "Come on. One cup of coffee can't hurt," he said the next week at Bible study.

"All right. *One* cup of coffee."

Three hours flew by as they ate pie, sipped coffee, and easily talked about their lives. Driving Janice home, Gerry kidded, "See, that wasn't too bad, was it?"

Janice laughed, "No, I guess you don't bite."

"Let's do it again next week."

When she lay in bed that night, Janice smiled to herself thinking about Gerry. Then she caught herself and stopped dead in her tracks. "Oh no, Lord! Not another charmer. Please, Father, lead me in this."

After a year of courting, Gerry took Janice in his arms and looking straight into her eyes, he said, "Janice, I love you. Will you please be my wife?"

Her heart thumped wildly. "Before we make any decisions, Gerry, we need to get premarital counseling."

"Of course. Why don't we ask Pastor Jim? He knows both of us."

Janice and Gerry began counseling with their pastor and he guided them through what it takes to have a godly marriage. "You know, we also have to talk through your pasts," he told them during one session. "Getting married at an older age means you both are walking into this marriage with extra baggage, and you need to clearly understand what each bag holds."

Finally, after many hours of counseling, Pastor Jim announced, "I think you two are ready." Relief filled Janice. Smiling at Gerry, she squeezed his hand as he sincerely thanked their pastor. "Your counsel has meant the world to us."

"Okay, Lord," Janice said in her prayer time that night. "Our pastor has given us the thumbs-up. I am taking this as Your leading. It does feel so good to have a godly man adore me. Thank You, Lord."

The first night of the honeymoon, she lay in their bed while Gerry snored soundly beside her. "Lord," she whispered, "something feels very wrong. When we made love, I felt violated. It felt so degrading. Am I just out of practice? I mean it's been over 20 years. Or is something really wrong here?"

Janice fell into a fitful sleep but the next day, Gerry waited on her hand and foot and she berated herself. *Get ahold of yourself, Janice. This man is different from the others. You have learned, for goodness sakes!*

Then a week after their honeymoon, Janice called Gerry to let him know she would be late getting home. When she couldn't reach him, she had an odd foreboding. "He's not going to like this." But as she set the receiver down, she lost herself in the flood of paperwork atop her desk.

When Janice got home later that night, Gerry snapped, "Where were you tonight?"

"I worked late. I tried to call you."

"Liar!" Gerry grabbed Janice's shoulders. "I went there. Your car wasn't even there."

"I parked around back. Let go of me, Gerry!" Janice struggled to get out of his grip.

In a fit of jealous rage, Gerry assaulted Janice.

Janice's marriage crumbled into pieces before her eyes that night. Her gut reaction on their wedding night was confirmed. Something was drastically wrong with Gerry.

Over the next several weeks, she learned just how bad it was. And she found herself, yet again, married to a "Tall, Dark, and Handsome" phony. This time was worse than any of the others because this man was dangerous. Janice discovered that Gerry had a whole set of sexual and drug addictions. And not only that, he was the most incredible con artist Janice had ever seen. He had everyone fooled. Their pastor. Their friends. And most of all, Janice.

Trying to save the marriage, she looked into all kinds of addiction interventions and programs. But Gerry refused to get help. After seeking guidance from her pastor, she knew there was only one way out. Divorce. For the third time in her life.

"How could I be so fooled?" Janice cried to Pastor Jim. "He seemed so sincere in his faith. We prayed together. He acted so loving to me. It was all a big sham!"

Pastor Jim shook his head. "I know, Janice. Some people are wolves in sheep's clothing. He deceived you, and Satan wants to have a heyday with this. Don't let him, Janice. Let God use it for good."

"How? How could He possibly use any of this for good?"

Grieving over this marriage, Janice wallowed in utter despondency. "I thought You were with me in this decision, Lord."

But God met her down in her despair. She gently heard Him beckoning her. *Janice, I can take all of you and use it for My glory—if you let Me. I can take your mistakes, your brokenness, your whole journey, and restore what was lost. I want to finish the work I have begun. But you need to let Me.*

"Lord, it is so hard. Satan wants me to hide in shame, to be weakened in Your work. Who am I to be doing ministry? What do I have to offer? Look at me!"

Yes. That is what he wants. In him there is only a crippling bondage to shame. In Me there is victory. Don't hide where you've been, Janice. Be vulnerable with others. And allow Me to use your life to show I am the Restorer for those who love Me.

Janice rose to His calling. Today she is the Women's and Spiritual Care Pastor at a large church. She gets opportunities every week to encourage other women who have made major mistakes. Just last week, she spoke to a large group on becoming a woman God can use.

"Ladies, I am here today as living proof that God is a Restorer. We all have a past. Some are more thickly plastered with blunders and boo-boos than others. But we all have them. Don't push your past under the carpet like we so often want to do. Your past is part of who you are. Allow God to use it. I know all too well how mistakes make you wanna run and hide. You see, I married the same man three times; he just looked different. We need to know that Satan has quite a bag of tricks and for most of us, he can trip us up with the same trick over and over again. He tripped me with phony Prince Charmings.

> *"Satan doesn't want us to forgive ourselves, but God does."—Janice*

‿

"I wish there was a big red button I could push that said, 'DO OVER.' But there isn't. Actually, there is something better because our God is not the God of three strikes and you're out. He is also not the God of only homecoming kings and queens. Rather He is the God of screw-ups, people who blow it again and again, people like you and me."

Janice also shares with the women how God is the Master of taking our big-time blotches and using them to mold us to be more like Him. Using Moses, David, and Paul as examples, she shows the women how God uses people with pasts—people who know the meaning of blowing it big time.

"He can use you, too," she beams. "If you let Him. Give Him your past. He has begun a work in you.

"Let Him complete it."

In Their Footsteps

"I have a hard time sharing myself with others but when I do, it is so freeing."

—Beth, 60

"God can use anything for a purpose. Many times we are being shown something and being strengthened to be used by God for something else later."

—Anonymous, 68

"God wants us to be vulnerable with our close friends, but Christians tend to put on a big front. Look at how vulnerable the apostle Paul was. He shared both his weaknesses and strengths."

—Anonymous

"Don't let trials break you but make a choice to believe that God is with you in the midst of them and will use them if you allow Him."

—Anonymous, 64

Strengthened Faith Summary

∾

All the stories in this book describe profound moments in individual journeys with God. Each story provides a glimpse into how God works in our ordinary, daily lives and how He provides us with choices to open ourselves up to Him all along the way.

The three women we chose for this chapter illustrate lives that experienced God's profound strength, grace, and restoration. Denise has learned to completely rely on God's promise for His mercy and strength every morning. Ihla drank in God's grace throughout her pilgrimage into widowhood. And Janice, like all of us, needed God's hand of restoration; she received it fully, allowing God to use her, mistakes and all.

These stories demonstrate how God yearns for a deep, intimate relationship with each one of us in which He can uphold us, walk with us, and love us. But the choice is ours. Do we allow Him in?

Why do you think some women are bitter at the end of their life and some women are joyful? How do you think you can prevent yourself from growing into a bitter old woman?

How do you currently pursue a relationship with God? What do your quiet times with God look like? What makes you feel closest to God?

Do you have any mistakes or sins in your life that you have closed off to God and others? What could Janice have done after her series of mistakes? What kind of person do you think she would be now if she had allowed shame to rule her?

What do you think the verse that Ihla clung to—"My grace is sufficient for you" (2 Corinthians 12:9)—means? Have you experienced God's grace in your life? How?

Suggestions:

1. Explore different ways to have a quiet time. Try going on a hike; finding a comfortable, relaxing spot to read your Bible with the phone off the hook; or listening to praise/worship music. Maybe spend time on your knees during part of your prayer time. Try different places and times of the day. After experimenting with your quiet time, was there one place and time that you felt most connected to God?

2. If you can arrange for several hours away, take a half-day trip to a favorite spot outdoors and sit alone with your journal and Bible. Alternate reading the Bible, writing in your journal, and sitting quietly.

3. Keep a journal of your prayers; date when and how God answers them.

4. Seek out a prayer partner you can meet with on a regular basis (once a week, once every two weeks, or even once a month). Try to keep the same prayer partner for several years so you can look back together and see how God has moved in your lives.

chapter six

where women walked . . .

through financial issues

Sandee

*She didn't have much money. In fact, her financial
situation was quite desperate. But it was there,
in the midst of her desperation, where Sandee learned a
powerful truth about God—a truth that changed the
course of her life and the lives of her daughters.*

Sandee stared through the murky Greyhound bus window as they rumbled down the empty highway. In the moonless night the bus seemed to be swallowed up by the blackness. She yawned and looked at her watch. Three A.M. and she still hadn't fallen asleep. She gently shifted her two sleeping daughters so she could stretch out her legs. Shauna, her youngest, woke up. "Mommy?"

"Yes, sugar. I'm right here," Sandee said, stroking her 10-year-old daughter's hair. "Everything's okay. You can go back to sleep." Within a few moments, Shauna's breathing became slow and deep again.

But everything wasn't okay. Sandee stared at the window. Her reflection caught the essence of her situation—a trembling young black woman, with tears streaming from grief-stricken eyes, cradling two trusting children.

So much unknown loomed in front of her. In just a few days she'd step into a strange city and start pounding the pavement looking for a job. She felt like a frightened child. *Oh, Lord,* she prayed, her voice hushed and thick. *Lord, I have never held a job in my life. I went from college to marriage to babies. You need to find me a job. Please, Lord . . . please, Father, help me.*

> *"There are times when I have had it out with God, but in the journey He has brought me on I have learned to trust Him with everything. Everything!"—Sandee, 60*

Charlynne, her 12-year-old, shifted the serene look on her face reminiscent of her father's. A fresh wave of pain hit Sandee. She winced. *Chuck.* She closed her eyes against the fresh tears. She had wanted so much to stay married. She had forgiven him for his affair but he didn't believe she really would. "No," Chuck said, unbending. "Every time I look at you, I'll feel judgment." He filed for divorce.

You know me, Lord. I can take a lot, Sandee prayed in spite of her exhaustion. *I'm trying to accept the divorce. But the one thing I can't accept is Chuck's disrespect of me. I just can't take that.*

All at once, something soft stirred in her spirit—like a whispered kiss. *Sandee. Wait. Be patient. One day he will honor you above all women.*

The gentle words filled her and the bus rocked her to sleep.

Three days later when the bus arrived in Denver, the girls went wild. Jumping up and down they hollered in unison, "We're here! We're here!"

"Girls, look." Sandee pointed out the window. "There's Uncle Mark."

The girls flew off the bus to be enveloped in a bear hug from their uncle. Sandee hugged her brother, then stepped back. "Thanks, Mark."

"Hey, no problem. Let's get your stuff."

Sandee waved her hand at a few boxes and three thin mattresses rolled up and tied with twine.

Mark looked at their belongings. "This is all you have?"

"Yep," nodded Sandee.

"Wow. You guys don't have much for moving across country. Well, pile in, everyone!" Mark said pointing to his truck.

All four squeezed into the cab, laughing at all the arms and legs trying to find places to fit.

Mark shifted while Shauna giggled and lifted her leg out of the way.

"So, Sandee, what's the plan?" Mark asked.

"Chuck's going to send me some money every month so I plan to get a part-time job and go to school. After I get situated and find a job, me and the girls will move into our own place." She paused, looking at her brother over the top of Shauna's head. "Does that sound okay?"

Mark reached over and squeezed his sister's hand. "Sounds perfect. You and the girls stay as long as you need to."

But Sandee's ideas didn't quite go the way she'd planned. The court-ordered support never came. Sandee postponed school and looked for a full-time job. She took the best offer and became a telemarketer working for minimum wage.

One morning, Sandee sat at her brother's kitchen table sipping her coffee before work. She took pencil and paper and began calculating their expenses. *It's going to be much tighter than I thought.* She tapped her pencil against the table, trying to see where they could cut even more.

Suddenly, she heard a noise upstairs. *That's weird,* she thought. Mark had already left for work and the girls were watching television downstairs.

Thump.

"Charlynne," she called out to her oldest, "stay down there with your sister until I tell you to come up."

Sandee tiptoed up the stairs then peered around the corner. A stark-naked woman strutted from Mark's bedroom to the bathroom.

Sandee quickly withdrew. She leaned against the wall, wondering what she should do. For the sake of her girls, there was only one thing she could do.

She marched down the stairs. Picking up the phone, she dialed her brother's office number. "Mark, give me a month."

"What are you talking about, Sandee?" he said, confused.

"I won't dictate what you do with your life," she said in a gentle but firm tone. "But I want one month where you don't bring any women home. During that month I'll find me and the girls a place to live." Sighing heavily she said, "I don't want the girls exposed to your lifestyle."

Finding a home proved to be a bigger challenge than Sandee bargained for. She looked everywhere for an apartment suitable for them. But wherever they went, they encountered obstacles.

One afternoon while she filled out the paperwork for a lease application, her pen ran out of ink. After several failed attempts to get it writing again, she threw the pen on the floor. "This is ridiculous anyway," she said to herself. "Who in the world is going to accept me? I've had a job for two weeks and I make a whopping $4.85 an hour. No one in his right mind would rent to me." Sandee squeezed her eyes shut. *Lord, I cannot focus on how incapable I am because I'll lose my mind. Help me to focus on You instead. Find a safe apartment for my girls and me. Please . . . I can't do this on my own.*

When Sandee got a phone call from an apartment manager, she couldn't believe her ears. "Girls!" she whooped. "Remember that apartment building? The one we really liked? They took us!" Grabbing both girls, she gave them a tight hug. "Thank You, Lord!"

Within a week they were settled in their new one-bedroom apartment. They didn't have much. No television, no radio, no furniture, not even dishes or silverware. But they didn't care. They sat on the kitchen floor slurping up spaghetti with plastic forks from paper plates. The girls giggled at the reddish-orange mess they made down their chins.

Sandee looked at her happy girls, worried about the next day. To get to her job now, it would take three buses and two hours. She'd have to leave the girls by themselves all day while she worked. She didn't want to leave them. But what else could she do?

The next morning, the sky looked like black ink when she locked the sleeping girls in their apartment and hurried off to catch the bus. She sat down on the bus and shuddered—more from fear than cold. As the bus pulled away from the curb, Sandee swallowed hard. She trembled. *I am terrified, Lord. I hate this. They are only 12 and 10. They're not safe!*

Sandee's shoulders heaved. She looked down and glared at the Bible in her lap. She felt angry toward God. *Why are You allowing this, Lord?* She didn't feel like reading her Bible or praying. But what else did she have? An out-of-control, desperate feeling rushed through her again. Tears splashed onto the book. She swiped the small, wet spots with her fingertips and took a deep breath, opening her Bible. *Lord,* she prayed silently, *You're all I have. Help me.*

She looked at the words and forced herself to read them. And slowly, they began to speak to her. She exhaled and her shoulders relaxed as she let the words fill her up. Oblivious to those around her, she began talking to her Bible. "I hear You, Lord. You want me to trust You. They're Your children and You're their Father."

The words of Scripture captivated her for the entire two hours she spent on the buses. A supernatural peace replaced her fear and anger. God's gentle voice penetrated her heart. *Sandee, I know you can't do this alone. So don't focus on what you can't do. Focus on Me. Remember? I am able to do all things. Give Me your family and allow Me to make a testimony beyond any testimony you could dream of. Will you let Me?*

By the time Sandee stepped off the bus her heart overflowed with peace. She sang praise hymns while she walked down the sidewalk, then practically floated into the gray glass office building. "Thank You, Father," she whispered as she settled at her desk.

Sandee made it her habit, after that first morning on the bus, to spend the commuting hours in prayer and studying her Bible. A lot of mornings she felt mad at God and she ranted and raved about her desperate financial situation. But no matter how big of a fit she threw, she always found peace when she read His Word.

Several weeks after they moved into their apartment, Sandee made arrangements to take the girls in for an interview at a private Christian school. The night before the interview Sandee called Chuck to ask about the missed child support payments. He delivered his lame excuses in a dry tone. When she told him she was looking into the girls' attending a private school, he scoffed. "Where are you going to get the money for that, Sandee? Certainly not from me."

Sandee hung up. Her shoulders sagged in defeat.

God, I'm totally ill-equipped to be doing this by myself. Chuck has money. I don't. Look at how we live, she prayed, looking around the bare apartment. *I'm overwhelmed, Lord. I only have You. Help me to know that You are all I need.*

The next morning before they left for the interview, Sandee held the girls' hands in a firm grip and bowed her head. "Lord, these are Your girls. This is the school You've led us to. If You want them there, You'll have to work out the finances."

After the girls completed their interviews and admittance tests, the school principal ushered them into his office. "Ms. Bodie," he said, turning his brown leather swivel chair toward her. "If your girls are admitted to this school, how will you pay for their tuition?"

> *"Believe Him for the impossible."—Sandee*

Sandee sat tall, her hands folded in her lap, and looked directly into the principal's eyes. "Sir, I make very little money and my ex-husband hasn't paid much child support. But my girls are excellent students. If you can help us with a scholarship, you'll not be disappointed. We will make you proud."

The principal swiveled his chair back and forth, fixing his gaze on Sandee. Then he said after a long pause, "I believe the Lord is saying that is exactly what we should do, Ms. Bodie."

To celebrate God's faithfulness, Sandee took the girls out for hot chocolate and sweet rolls. "You need to realize what God did today, girls," she said, pouring cream into her coffee. "He is teaching us He has no limits." Setting her spoon down, she reached across the table and cupped both of their chins. "Now you both look at me." When she had their full attention, she continued. "Remember this one thing—don't let this world limit you. Not now. Not ever. People are not qualified to tell you what you can or can't do. There is only One who is qualified. Your Heavenly Father."

The girls blinked at their mom. "Okay. We'll remember," answered Charlynne for both of them and then took another giant bite of her sweet roll.

Sandee's words to the principal about her daughters were true. Sandee's two, poor, black daughters took their private school by storm. Charlynne obtained a perfect grade point average, won countless awards for speech and journalism, and evangelized her way through school. The homecoming queen received Christ as a result of Charlynne's witness. Shauna was class president three years in a row, won athletic awards, and was known by her classmates as a powerful prayer warrior.

Ten years later the phone rang late one evening in Sandee's apartment. As she put the receiver to her ear, she heard Charlynne's voice falter between sniffles. "M-om," she uttered a broken sob, "my English professor says I'm not cut out for journalism. She says I don't have what it takes. She wants me to drop her class."

"You listen to me, Char." Sandee spoke with a steady voice. "What have I taught you?"

"I know, Mom. She's not qualified."

"That's right. She's not. This is where God has led you. Right?"

"Right."

"And He is the only one qualified for you to listen to. You hear me?"

Charlynne heard her mother. She stayed in class. And later she graduated magna cum laude with a degree in journalism and went to work as a journalist for the lead press secretary at the White House. While everyone around them continually voiced their surprise at the

> "It is not about my plan for my life but His plan for my life."—Sandee

girls' accomplishments and awards, Sandee never felt surprised. "I once was a scared little mommy," she explains. "But in my desperation I came to know my God. And He is limitless. After all, He is the one who walks on water. We shouldn't be surprised by His hand in our lives."

Epilogue

The night before Charlynne graduated from high school Chuck flew out for his daughter's big day. Walking into the graduation ceremony with a camera dangling from a strap around his neck, he stopped in his tracks and shook his head. "Sandee, I fought you every step of the way when it came to a private school for these girls. But I look around here and am so thankful the girls were kept in this place."

"Me too," said Sandee, smiling up at him.

Taking her by the arm, he looked with sincerity into her eyes. "I never again want to be the reason for any pain or suffering in your life. I have come to realize you are an incredible woman. And I want you to know that I honor and respect you more than you could ever imagine."

Now Sandee stopped too. She didn't try to hold back the tears. But she looked at Chuck and said with tenderness in her voice, "Thank you."

As they sat down waiting for the graduation ceremony to begin, Sandee couldn't hold back her grin as she remembered her desperate plea on that Greyhound bus so many years earlier. *That's my God,* she thought. *That's my limitless God.*

In Their Footsteps

"We need to trust Him with our finances but this is very hard to do because our finances make us feel secure. I knew a woman who lived completely by faith and she had the most amazing walk with God I have ever seen. She trusted Him with every need she had."
          —*Cathy, 52*

"I have learned to not underestimate God."
          —*Jody, 67*

"I learned that a relationship with God is more important than things. I also learned to expect the unexpected from God. That He is who He is, and I can't change that by wishful thinking or prayers or anything. He will do what He will do when He decides to do it. I had to learn to be grateful for that. I learned to fall on my face and be grateful. To trust when I couldn't understand. To hold on to God."

> —*Cathy, 50, a single mother of three children, who at times had no money for groceries. Sometimes all she had to feed them was popcorn. She also volunteered to work in a soup kitchen. Afterward, they would give her a bag of groceries to help her through the week.*

Barb

During her husband's time of unemployment,
Barb chose to build him up and praise him for his
wisdom, talents, and creativity. She also learned to trust
God for her security and for her future.

"Hi, Ken," Barb said cheerfully when her husband walked in the front door around noon. "I just made myself a turkey sandwich. If I'd known you were coming home for lunch, I would have made you one too. Do you want one?" she asked as she rubbed the mustard off her fingers onto a napkin.

She went over to him to give him a peck on the cheek but stopped in her tracks when she looked at him and saw his red-rimmed eyes.

"Ken, what's wrong? You look . . . exhausted," Barb said.

"Barb, I have some bad news," Ken answered.

Ken reached out and held her hand, then led her to a chair in the kitchen. After sitting down, Ken took off his glasses, placed them on the table, and rubbed his eyes.

"Barb, as of this moment, I'm 50 years old and unemployed. The company went out of business today. I'm not sure what all happened. But there's absolutely nothing we can do now. I knew something was wrong at work, but I had no idea how serious the situation had become." As he spoke, sorrow, like a dark cloud, covered Ken's face. He looked deflated, as if someone had just belted him in the stomach. Sadness for him filled her as she realized his dreams and years of hard work had just vanished into thin air. For the past five years he had slaved endless hours and invested all of their savings into this company. Devastation was written all over his face.

"When I got to work this morning, we were told something BIG was going to happen today. Around 11:30 we gathered in the conference room for an announcement. A man from the bankruptcy court came in and matter-of-factly stated that they were taking possession of the company. He ordered us to vacate the premises immediately. We couldn't take anything! I couldn't even go back into my office and get the pictures of our family. After we left they were going to change all the locks."

> *"Coping in a crisis depends upon many things . . . attitude, having a solid and positive support system around you, and being real. Allow yourself to feel what you feel and express those feelings and struggles."—Barb, 60*

⟨ဿ

A confusing mixture of helplessness, anger, and sorrow coursed through Barb's body. "Oh, Ken, I am so sorry. I know how hard you've worked to build this company," she said as tears trickled down her cheeks. Ken gently wiped away her tears and dabbed at his own eyes.

"I'll just have to start looking for a new job. Barb, our investment is gone. We probably won't ever see a penny of the money. I'm so sorry. We also need to immediately start cutting our expenses. We've got to live on a tight budget, at least for a while," Ken said.

"We've lived on budgets before. I know I'm not very good at that, but we'll be okay." She took a deep breath. "I'll cancel our dinner reservations for our anniversary tomorrow night. We can go out for a cheap dinner instead."

The next night, sitting at a sticky booth in a fast-food restaurant, they attempted to enjoy their evening together as they reminisced about previous anniversaries. Barb tried to not think about the wads of ABC (already been chewed) gum clinging to the underside of the table. *This isn't where I expected to spend our anniversary*, she thought. But Ken mattered more than anything in the world to her. He needed her to be positive and to lift him out of his dreary mood.

"Granted, we lost our retirement and his job went away, but I am so grateful that Ken was diligent in working toward being debt free. One of the biggest struggles throughout our marriage had been being on a budget versus not being on a budget. At this time in our lives, I was so grateful for Ken's foresight."—Barb

"Ken, remember four years ago, for our 25th anniversary, how you surprised me with a remarriage? That was one of the best anniversaries ever. I'll never forget redoing our wedding and our vows to each other in front of our friends and children," Barb said, trying to lift his spirits.

"Yeah, that was great," Ken muttered, staring out the window at the cars rushing by. A slight smile came and went.

"And then there was the year we lost all our money," she joked.

"When was that?" he asked.

"Yesterday," she chuckled, causing Ken to break into a grin and actually laugh.

"Oh yeah, how could I forget? This will be one to remember," he added as he reached across the table and gave her hand a gentle, reassuring squeeze.

"Ken, we've been through this before. God has been so faithful and He will be faithful to us again. You have so many gifts and talents. I know you will be able to find a new job. I'm not worried about that. Besides, I've got a good job at the church. At least we'll still have health insurance and some income."

"I know. I just feel terrible about losing all of our retirement money."

"You know how I feel about retirement. I never imagined us as a retired couple that traveled abroad and played golf. We both love working with people and helping people. I don't care about the money. I care about you and I love you," Barb said as she clung to his hand and looked deeply into his eyes.

"Thanks, sweetheart," Ken said, voice choking with emotion. "I love you too. I trust God will use this in our life somehow. I know He will."

The day after their 29th anniversary, Ken began his search for a new job. This task took a tremendous toll on him. He worked long hours sending out résumés and seeking interviews. Meanwhile, Barb worked at their church as the Director of Caring Ministry. She spent most of her days reading files about families needing assistance and interviewing people in crisis. She and her team then decided how to allocate services and assistance to those people. *How ironic,* she thought, *now I'm in the same boat as most of these folks. But, Lord, thank You for this job; thank You that we still have benefits and insurance. Thank You that I'm doing what I love to do. Please guide Ken as he searches for work.*

> *"Be your husband's encourager. There will be plenty of other places outside your home for him to have discouragers."*
> *—Barb*

Together they developed and stuck to a rigid budget—something Barb always fought having to do. But now they didn't have a choice. When it came to purchasing clothes for themselves or anything for the house, they just didn't do it. Instead of buying gifts for their family, they made things. A date night consisted of walking the mall, window-shopping, and then sometimes splitting a giant cinnamon roll for a treat. They even resigned to giving each other haircuts. One time, Ken actually frosted Barb's hair—and he did a great job with it.

As Ken's unemployment continued, Barb watched his self-esteem shrink. She knew he needed her to be his encourager. She went out of her way to praise him for his talents, his wisdom, and his creativity. When he verbally beat himself up for the decisions he felt he made, she would build him up and remind him of his many successes.

> *"Encourage your husband to take care of himself. Proper diet, rest, exercise."—Barb*

"Barb, I'm so discouraged I can't even pray," Ken confessed one morning on their daily prayer walk. "I never imagined it would be so hard and take so long to find a job that I would be excited about."

❧

"That's okay, Ken. I'll just pray this morning. You've been doing everything possible to find a job, I know that," Barb said.

"Well, I did find a job as a quality control officer at the new airport under construction," Ken said. "Basically, what I would do is stand around in the cold and look over the shoulders of workers who don't want me there. I'm thinking of taking it; at least it is some income."

"Is that what you want to do?" Barb asked.

"No, not for the long haul, but as a temporary job, it pays pretty well. Barb, we need the money. I'll do anything to feel useful and help carry our financial burden. I know it's been hard on you to do that alone."

"Well, that's probably a good idea right now. I guess you'll be needing some warm snow boots; we'd better go get you some before you start," Barb said.

For the next four months, Ken stood around in the freezing cold of winter in his new snow boots, overseeing construction workers. Barb fixed him lunches daily and continually praised him for his willingness to do whatever it took to make some money. He experienced emotional and spiritual ups and downs—good days and bad days. And Barb became his constant companion and encourager. She felt proud of him for taking a job he didn't love, yet she encouraged him to keep dreaming and searching for something more fulfilling.

Over the span of four years, Ken took advantage of several job opportunities. None were in his field of expertise and all were temporary. Ken decided to start a business more closely related to his background of computer consulting—a business that continues to provide a stable income. This allows him to be his own boss and work at home. Also, the flexibility makes it possible for him to do the work that brings him the most joy and fulfillment—serving others through their church.

Ken's consulting jobs come and go, but Barb doesn't worry about their financial future. Through her husband's time of unemployment she's learned that security doesn't come from financial stability. Her security rests in trusting God for their future.

> *"Encourage your husband to have someone to talk with in addition to you. And make sure you have encouragers in your life."*—**Barb**

Barb and Ken kissed their retirement good-bye but found security in God and in their relationship with each other. They both enjoy working and plan to serve God and others as long as possible.

"God brought us together those many years ago. He brought together two individuals who brought into our marriage unique gifts. God designed us to build each other up. Over the years, we both have had opportunities to build each other up or tear each other down. Most times, we've built each other up. Throughout our marriage I have believed in Ken. I believed in him in the midst of his job loss. I believe he is very gifted, wise, and creative. And I believe we have an exciting adventure before us."

In Their Footsteps

"God has always provided for our needs. And as my husband and I look toward the end of our lives, we trust that will be true even though right now the stock market teeters and wars rage."
— *Pat, 72*

"My dad was stuck in a job that he never really enjoyed and at times, he was miserable to be around. When I married, I decided I wanted my husband to always have a job that he enjoyed. So, as he desired to switch jobs, I always encouraged him to do it—especially if it seemed like something exciting and rewarding to him. Our income fluctuated but that didn't matter to me as much as living with a happy, fulfilled person, and he's done the same for me."
—*Mary Jane, 68*

"When unemployment came, we tightened our belts and sought God's guidance. Living through the Great Depression has probably been a blessing. It's no big deal to give up sodas, chips, movies, eating out, and other things because life is so much more than any of those things. In our last unemployment experience it was wonderful to see that we did not have to cut even one commitment to our church, a missionary, or other agencies. God is good!"
—*Janet, 71*

"If a man can love what he's doing and love his family, that's a blessing."
—*Barbara, 60*

Hazel

*Through unexpected resources, Hazel and her
husband went from nearly losing their family farm
to having more money than they'd ever dreamed.
Hazel shares the importance of the discipline of giving—
no matter what your circumstances.*

Hazel stood in the dusty barnyard wiping the sweat and dirt from her forehead. She had just finished milking the cows and was about to look in the chicken coop to see if any of the hens had laid any eggs. As she looked around, worry crept into her heart. *Oh, Lord, I know times have been tough before, but this is really getting serious. I love this farm and don't want to lose it. Please help us get out of debt,* Hazel prayed as she gathered a few freshly laid, warm, light brown-colored eggs and gingerly placed them in her basket. *Lord, You know we've given this farm to You; it's Your land, but we love it. I can't bear the thought of leaving here.* She wiped away a tear that tried to spill down her face.

The farm had been in Hazel's family since 1891. In fact, she was born in this house in 1926. She and her husband, Dean, had farmed the land for 58 years. And during those years they had experienced numerous ups and downs. Lately, there were more downs than ups.

But Dean loved farming—it's what he knew and loved to do. And Hazel loved the land. On it they grew potatoes, corn, sugar beets, beans, and other produce. They also kept cattle and sheep and sold them at the market. But it was a rough life. Years of carrying heavy buckets filled with corn and water, and weeding the fields day after day, put permanent aches in Hazel's back. It was also rough financially. Sometimes the crops were hailed out, the cattle market went up and down, and other factors out of their control made each year's income unpredictable. Many times, they had to rely on this land for sustenance. For food they often ate the vegetables they grew, butchered their own chickens, and drank the milk from their cows. It was a hard life.

The erratic income made it difficult to make ends meet. When Hazel was a young mom, she went back to school and earned a master's degree in teaching. For 23 years she taught school to pay for their children's college educations.

Early in their marriage, Hazel and Dean made a commitment to give the first portion of whatever income they had toward the Lord's work. Even though finances were often very tight, they *always* gave no matter what. From every single paycheck they ever received, the first thing they did was give to their church, to missionaries, or to whatever need they felt most impressed to provide for.

But during the previous year, the debts piled up and threatened to sink them. It was 1983; the cattle market had dropped again, and their potatoes had rotted in the dugout. The love and attachment Hazel felt for her land and home caused an ache in the pit of her stomach at the thought of losing it. All she could do was pray. *Lord, I know You are in control. You've always helped us before; please help us again.*

That afternoon as she stood at the sink rinsing vegetables for dinner, she heard the squeaky screen door open and slam shut. Then she heard the familiar footsteps of Dean coming into the kitchen to find her.

"Hi, Momma," Dean said, and then he came up close behind her and gave her a kiss on the back of her head. "I had an interesting conversation today. On my way home from the cattle market, I stopped at the coffee shop in town for a cup, and this man came up to me and asked if I knew of any land where he could set up an oil drilling rig. I told him we had some land. After we talked, he was really interested. It looks like we might start drilling for oil out here."

Hazel couldn't believe her ears. "What? Oil on our farm? When? Who is this guy? Do you really think they'll find anything?"

"I knew you'd be full of questions, so I invited him over to talk through the details with us. Then we can pray about it and decide what to do," Dean said.

After learning about the process and agreeing upon the royalties, Hazel and Dean signed a contract with a company to drill for oil on their farm. They watched as the platform with an oil rig appeared on their landscape. Then one day the young man that monitored the drilling made his way through the chickens in the front yard and knocked on Hazel's door.

"Hi, Hazel," he said smiling from ear to ear. "We've struck oil!"

Again, Hazel was speechless. *I can't believe we've had this resource under our feet all these years,* she mused. When Dean came home that afternoon, they prayed and rejoiced together at the Lord's blessing. The oil brought them enough earnings to pay off all their debts. They no longer had any fear of losing their home. She was told that the oil reserves would probably run out in about 15 years, but today, over 20 years later, the well's still

> *"We always tithed, no matter what. Leviticus 27:30 says, 'A tithe of everything from the land, whether grain from the soil or fruit from the trees, belongs to the LORD; it is holy to the LORD.' So, we always gave to the Lord first, and He always gave to us when we needed it."—Hazel*

producing. As always, Hazel and Dean tithed the first portion of every dollar they earned from the oil and continue to do so with each monthly royalty check they receive.

Then, about 17 years later, another unexpected opportunity fell into their laps. The area around them had begun to attract developers. Houses popped up everywhere. But one thing every developer needs is water rights. Thanks to his wise foresight, Hazel's father had bought shares of water from the nearby reservoir. After his death Hazel inherited the farm, which included 260 acres and a more-than-adequate supply of water shares.

One day, their friend Glen dropped by. He knew their lives as farmers had been rough. So he offered them a proposal they couldn't refuse. After some polite conversation, he asked, "Have you ever considered selling some of your water shares? I think I know someone who would buy them from you."

"We've thought about it," Hazel explained. "Last time we checked, they were worth about $400 per acre foot; it just didn't seem worth it to sell. That really wasn't enough to help us at the time. How much are they worth now?"

"Well, times have certainly changed! Now, they're worth about $10,000 per acre foot," Glen explained. Hazel's and Dean's jaws dropped.

"We had no idea," Hazel uttered.

Together, they decided to sell 100 shares and buy some cheaper water from a nearby ditch system. That way, they could continue to farm the land and not let it turn into a barren wasteland. This decision to sell netted them one million dollars.

"We had a million dollars for a day," Hazel jokes. "After paying taxes and capital gains, we ended up with $890,000. I couldn't believe it. That's more money than I will ever need. I'd lived so long with so little, I really didn't care about money that much. But it did make my life a bit easier. Now, I don't have to worry about paying our increasing medical bills. But truly, the best part of it all is the joy of giving money away."

Hazel and Dean devoted the firstfruits of their windfall to the Lord's work. They prayed for opportunities to give money to people who needed it. They gave to their children and other family members, and they set up college funds for their grandchildren. They gave money to missionaries, single moms, medical missions, and orphans in Africa. They gave money to a family who had a child with special needs. "It was so exciting. I felt such joy every time I wrote a check that I knew would help someone who needed it."

They gave money to repair a Christian broadcasting tower that was knocked out by a hurricane in a developing country. They also donated money to build water wells and purchase seeds to be planted in other poor countries. "It's wonderful to receive letters that tell about how many people in poor countries are now getting water due to these wells and how many are learning to farm their own land. To be a small part of that is incredible. When you have a love for the land, like Dean and I do, it feels wonderful to help others learn to provide for themselves."

> *"Be sure the Lord gets His share. Whatever you do, give to the Lord first. Don't give to Him after paying all your bills and buying things for yourself. Make the first check you write after every paycheck be for something to help someone else. Then see what you have left to pay your bills with."—Hazel*

People thought they were crazy because they didn't do much for themselves. "Everyone asked me if we were going to build a big house in town, and I always said, 'No, why would I? I am happy here.'" Hazel adds, "We did replace the windows that had been in our house since 1949 with new storm windows. We bought a nice big table and matching hutch for our dining room. The hutch has glass windows so I can display all the pretty things I got as wedding gifts."

Hazel and Dean continue to look for opportunities to give and reap the benefits of joy and peace in cheerfully giving away what the Lord has given them. "We've always tithed first, but we often give much more beyond that," Hazel says. "As it says in Psalm 50:10-12, the 'cattle on a thousand hills' are His, and 'the world is mine, and all that is in it.' After all, it all belongs to Him."

In Their Footsteps

"The first thing every month that we write a check for is a tithe to our church. Then everything else we give is above and beyond that amount. For years, whenever we have been asked to give, we both separately pray about it. Then we write down the amount we feel led to give. Ninety-nine times out of 100, we come up with the exact same amount."
        —*Jeannie, 58*

"God never ceases to surprise me with His extravagance."
        —*Ruth, 65*

"I've found it truly is more of a blessing to give than to receive. Knowing that you're helping someone else brings a certain amount of satisfaction. I think that's what we're supposed to do—give to others and you'll be surprised at the blessings you receive."
        —*Jennifer, 71*

"When I was a teenager, my mother would know someone sick in bed. She would tell me to go over and help them and not to accept a penny for it. She taught me the importance of helping others. Now, when I help someone else, I feel so much joy that I feel like I'm up in the clouds flying around like an angel. When I go to bed at night, I feel so good because I know I've helped others."
        —*Elizabeth, 95, who has received numerous awards*
            for her commitment to volunteerism during the past
            55 years

"A heart filled with God leads to hands open and able to give good gifts. Godly giving defines, disciplines, and blesses the giver and the receiver."
        —*Linda, 66*

Financial Issues Summary

捠

A majority of Americans list finances as the number one issue in life that causes them stress.

Why? Perhaps it's because most people base their security on their ability to provide financially for themselves and their families today and in the future. It's not wrong to plan ahead, but sometimes unplanned circumstances deplete that treasured financial security. Poof, and it can be gone!

Many of the women we interviewed lived through incredible times of financial hardship. Like the women in this chapter: Sandee, who daily lived within inches of poverty, or Barb, whose husband lost his job and their retirement money, or Hazel, who went from rags to riches. But all of these women learned to put their trust in something bigger and more certain than money—they put their trust in God. Ultimately, He is the one in control of the future, and most importantly, He loves and cares about those who love Him.

How has God met your needs in times of financial hardship? List those times in a journal as a reminder of His provision. Refer to this list of blessings often.

How would you feel if you lost all your money, your home, your lifestyle?

What are you modeling to your children about finances?

Are you overspending according to your income? If so, why? List three specific steps you can take to immediately decrease your spending.

Are you a cheerful giver of your money? Do you regularly give to charity?

What are your thoughts and ideas about retirement?

Suggestions:

1. Create a budget and stick to it. Seek an older woman and ask her to hold you accountable to your budget. Get tips from her on practical ways to save money rather than spend it.
2. Cut up one credit card today!
3. Pray for God to give you His perspective on money matters. Pray for the ability to trust Him with your daily needs and your future.
4. If you know people who struggle financially, do something to help them. Take them all the ingredients to make brownies or fill a bag with groceries and anonymously leave it at their door.
5. Take the children of a struggling family to buy them a new pair of shoes or outfit. Back-to-school supplies are often difficult for struggling families to provide for their children.
6. Team up with an older couple or person to adopt a family who may have ongoing needs. Invite them over for dinner or take them out. Something as simple as a delivered pizza and a rented movie can be a great treat.

chapter seven

where women walked . . .

through depression

Amy

Being molested as a little girl set the stage for Amy's lifelong battle with depression. Although she had a deep personal relationship with God, she couldn't seem to overcome her sorrow. And being around Christians just made her feel worse. But finally, after receiving medical help, she saw through the dense fog and realized that a relationship with God wasn't enough. She needed professional help. And God guided her toward that help.

Six-year-old Amy sat on the freshly mowed crabgrass in the front yard, her pigtails bouncing up and down as she maneuvered her plastic zoo animals in and out of the makeshift miniature swimming pool she had just constructed.

"Amy, come on," called her mother.

"I don't want to go. I want to stay here and play." Her bottom lip stuck out.

"Amy, I have to get something for dinner tonight. Come on. Let's go."

"Mrs. Edwards," interrupted 16-year-old Kenneth, the boyfriend of Amy's older sister, Annamarie. "It's okay. I'm going to be working on my car for at least another hour. Amy can stay here with me."

"Are you sure, Kenneth? Okay, Amy, be a good girl," her mom hollered over her shoulder as she climbed into her station wagon.

Amy turned her attention back to her toys, submerging a family of hippos underwater.

A few minutes after Amy's mom left, Kenneth walked into the house beckoning the little girl to join him. "Hey, cutie. Come here. I want to show you something."

Amy flung her animals down and ran inside. She felt so special whenever Kenneth paid attention to her. "Hey, darling," he directed Amy into the guest bedroom. "Lay down on the bed with me."

> *"I thought there was something in me that was so bad that brought about him doing all that to me. It was my fault. I was just sure of it."—Amy, 57*

Amy lay down, smiling up at Kenneth. But when he pulled down her shorts and underwear she froze. Something was wrong. Her young mind started to race. *What is he doing? This is wrong.* When Kenneth put his mouth where no one ever touched, she became paralyzed. Terrified to move. Terrified to speak. TERRIFIED.

After a few minutes, Kenneth abruptly got up, grumbled, "I'm sorry," and left the room. But Amy just sat on the yellow daffodil bedspread, totally numb. Her thoughts spiraled in confusion. *"Mommy! What did he just do to me? I want my mommy. Mommy, help."* She squeezed her eyes shut, hoping that what just happened would go away. But it didn't.

When Amy's mom got home, she began frying meat and onions for dinner while Amy tiptoed to her room and shut the door. *If I tell her, she'll think I did something wrong.* Amy felt like throwing up. *Did I?*

At dinner Amy's mom looked at her with a furrowed brow. "What's wrong with you?"

"Nothing."

Amy never looked up once through dinner. After picking at her food, she asked to be excused.

In bed that night she couldn't fall asleep. *My parents love Kenneth. My sister loves Kenneth. He couldn't have done anything wrong. It must be me.*

Amy's own personal prison began that day and Kenneth's molestation continued. Two years later, when her sister married Kenneth, Amy stood stoically at the altar as the junior bridesmaid, while tormenting thoughts raged inside her. *Now that they're married, I will never let anything happen again.*

A few weeks after the wedding Kenneth dropped by the house and Amy exited out the back door, calling to her mom that she would be over at Becky's house. *I've just got to stay away from him,* she told herself while walking to Becky's. Amy began distancing herself from not only Kenneth but from everyone else. She became a master at living in two worlds. The world at school where she played the extrovert, fun-loving, happy girl, and the other world where a deep agonizing sorrow festered inside her.

One day in seventh grade after putting on a bubbly, carefree face for her friends, she came home exhausted and did the usual—walked straight to her room, shut the door, and fell onto her bed. *This is the best part of my day,* thought Amy. *I don't have to talk to anyone or deal with anything.* She rolled over and hit the PLAY button on her radio, letting herself sink into the sad, lonely place that consumed her.

Despair trailed Amy through high school and into college. During her junior year at Florida University she saw a doctor who halfheartedly listened to her mental health battle and then prescribed a large bottle of tranquilizers. Walking home from the doctor's office, she felt the burden of life bearing down on her so heavily that it was difficult to breathe. Her steps were slow, her mind foggy. She had a date that night and they were going dancing. *I don't know if I can keep doing this,* she thought. Even the idea of dancing, her very favorite pastime, seemed like a monumental chore.

She collapsed onto her bed when she got home and escaped the world in sleep. When she woke, she mustered up the strength to get dressed and go on the date. The dancing and socializing numbed the pain for the evening, but afterward, the intense sorrow swallowed her once again. In the dark hallway of her apartment she sank to the floor as the familiar all-consuming despair covered her like a thick blanket. *Is this all there is?* she cried.

With all hope snuffed out she dragged herself up and walked to the kitchen sink, pulled down a large glass, and filled it to the brim with water. She walked into her room and picked up the bottle of tranquilizers. *I can't live like this any more. I don't want to do this any more. I want to end the pain.*

As she sat down on her bed, she began methodically unscrewing the lid. *I'll just take the whole bottle and be done with it.* She began pouring pills into her left palm but all at once, she felt a large, gentle hand resting on her arm. She looked behind her—no one was there. Closing her eyes, she concentrated. *Yes. I feel it. A definite hand is on my arm.* She looked down at the bottle and shook her head.

"I can't do this," she gasped and dropped the bottle onto the floor.

Amy was unsure what to do next. When her eyes rested on the forgotten Bible crammed at the back of her desk, her mind flashed back to that precious moment with her mother when she was seven years old and accepted Christ into her heart.

Snuggled together in an overstuffed chair, Amy had asked her mom, "How do you know you believe in Jesus?"

"Well, sweetie, it's a choice. Everyone gets to decide whether they believe Jesus is who He said He is. If you make a choice to believe in Him, then He lives in your heart forever."

"Do some people not believe?"

"Sure. Lots of people don't believe."

"Not me, Mom." Amy shook her head with determination.

"Amy, do you want to ask Jesus into your heart and make Him your personal Savior?"

"Yes."

"Okay. Pray this prayer with me," instructed her mom.

As Amy thought now about that prayer, she realized that even though on that day she accepted Jesus into her heart, she had never lived out that prayer. *It's just like Mom and Dad,* she thought. *They professed a faith, had accepted Christ as their Savior, but their lives lacked any intimate relationship with Him.*

"Okay, God," Amy weakly announced. "I'll try one more time. But if this is all there is in life, I don't want it. There's too much pain. You're my last chance. I'm going to give my life totally to You—but if You don't have the answers, I'm outta here."

With this last-ditch declaration Amy picked up her Bible and opened it. Staring down at the first words her eyes fell upon, she felt God speak to her:

Do not fear, for I am with you; do not be dismayed, for I am your God. I will strengthen you and help you; I will uphold you with my righteous right hand. (Isaiah 41:10)

Amy let the words wash over her while a single ray of hope flickered inside her heart. When she woke the next morning, her spirit felt lifted and she resolved to find a church. As she grew as a Christian, there was some relief to her depression. She felt hope for tomorrow and was able to wake up not dreading the day. She dated several guys and, when she was 23, met Tom, a new guy at church. They fell in love and got married.

Several years later after their first child was born, depression slapped Amy in the face again with a vengeance. Feeding Gracie early one morning in the rocking chair, Amy looked out the window with tears streaming down her cheeks. When Tom walked into the nursery to kiss her good-bye, she felt embarrassed that he'd found her crying again. "Tom, I'm so sorry. I don't know what is wrong with me. I should be so joyful. We have this beautiful baby girl." She choked on her emotions and couldn't stop the tears.

"It's going to be okay, sweetheart," he soothed his wife. But Amy knew the truth was that he felt lost and unsure about how to help her. Then one evening a few weeks later, when Tom got home from work, the colicky baby was crying, the dishes lay stacked in the sink, and Amy hadn't even dressed for the day. As Tom wrapped his arms around her, Amy brokenly wept. "I must not even be a Christian. Something must be wrong with my faith because I shouldn't be like this."

In bed that night, Tom looked over at his troubled wife. "I think it would be good for you to have someone to talk to. Someone who has been through postpartum depression and who understands."

Numb, Amy nodded. The next day in desperation, she picked up the phone and called her pastor's wife, Cynthia. When Cynthia arrived a few days later for a visit, Amy greeted her at the door with a surge of relief. "I'm so glad you were able to come over," she gushed.

Amy made them both tea and they sat down in the living room to talk. "It's been a long six months and I feel like I need to talk to someone who's had children," Amy began. "I have just come to the end of my rope with the colic and lack of sleep. I mean, I always thought having a child would be such a Hallmark moment." Amy stopped for a second because she felt so vulnerable. But taking a deep breath, she made herself go on. "But I can't seem to get it together. I feel so overwhelmed and blue sometimes. There are days when I think to myself 'I CAN'T DO THIS!'"

Sipping her decaffeinated tea, Cynthia looked at Amy with pursed lips. "Well, I'm sorry. I just can't relate to you at all. I was never like this when I had my babies. They *were* Hallmark moments." She set her tea down and crossed her legs. "In fact, I always treasured that time when they were so little and needed me so much. I knew my children were gifts from God so I counted every minute of raising them as a blessing. Maybe you

> *"In Hosea God says, 'My people are destroyed for lack of knowledge.' For so long I didn't have the knowledge."*—Amy

should try that. Don't complain so much if the baby fusses here and there. And remember, she's God's gift to you so be joyful about motherhood."

Amy curled up in a ball on the bed after Cynthia left. *I'm hopeless,* she thought. *There's something wrong with me.*

The next morning she forced herself out of bed. *Just make it through today, Amy,* she urged herself. Everyday tasks felt like a monumental effort. When she crawled into bed that night, she pulled the covers over her head, dreading the next day.

The depression continued to saturate every area of her life. Finally, two years after her second daughter was born, Amy went in for a physical exam and confided in her doctor. After a battery of questions he prescribed medication that would boost her seratonin levels. The medication felt like a breath of fresh air lifting the fog from her mind.

With a new clarity of mind Amy began to think and pray about receiving professional counseling to help her cope with her depression. For so many years she had believed that since she was a Christian and knew the Great I AM, the True Counselor, she shouldn't need professional help. But now she reconsidered her thinking and decided to see if a counselor could help her understand her depression. After finding a well-respected Christian counselor, Amy began a six-year journey of painful yet liberating work.

> *"Just because you forgive someone doesn't mean you have to start spending time with them. I forgave Kenneth but still knew I could never be close to him."—Amy*

"You are not only a victim of sexual molestation, but you suffer from post-traumatic stress disorder," explained her counselor. Amy began to understand so many things about herself and the bizarre way she behaved at times.

During one session Amy confided that on occasion, she experienced severe waves of panic about her daughters. "It is so weird." She shook her head talking to her counselor. "This week I was in the middle of vacuuming and all of a sudden, I panicked and had to drive to their school to make sure they were okay."

"There is a name for that," gently explained her counselor. "It's called hypervigilance. And a lot of times it happens to people who have been victimized—especially when they have children who are around the age they were when victimization took place."

Part of Amy's work included sharing with her sister and brother-in-law the memories from so long ago. Amy summoned all her courage and met with each of them individually. With written notes in her lap, she recounted all her painful experiences as a small child. Kenneth listened to everything Amy had to say without speaking a word. When she finished he admitted to every accusation and asked for her forgiveness. When it was all over, Amy felt like a boulder had been lifted off her shoulders. She could never retrieve what had been lost but she could heal, overcome, and move forward with her life.

By going through therapy, Amy felt deliverance from living under the suffocating vapor of depression. During this time her heart also began growing a burden for other Christians who had bought into the falsehood that she had. "It kills me that as Christians, we have these warped beliefs about getting help. We think we should just be able to walk out of our pain if we are walking closely to God. We put such a stigma on counseling and view it as a weakness or that something must be wrong with a person's faith if they need counseling."

> *"We are called to be overcomers and sometimes, to overcome a trauma in your life, it takes counseling."—Amy*

Today, as a licensed therapist, Amy is able to assure her clients that counseling is sometimes an essential ingredient in the healing process. Counselors can provide clarity, insight, and wisdom into what a person is feeling and why they are feeling that way.

"Professionals can lead people through their trauma and help them integrate it into their lives slowly so it is no longer this paralyzing event, but a memory," explains Amy to new clients. "God doesn't want us to walk in ignorance but knowledge. And, in certain cases, it is a counselor who can give that knowledge."

"And I know this firsthand," shares Amy. "Lack of knowledge about what I was feeling and experiencing almost killed me. Literally."

In Their Footsteps

"Depression leaves you feeling like you are drowning. The ones I hurt the most were those closest to me as I desperately tried to find someone, something to help alleviate the emotional pain. For a woman in the darkness of depression, her best friends are faithful friends."
—*Eileen, 44, who was sexually abused as a child*

"The darkness of depression leaves you feeling utterly abandoned by God. It is truly a test of faith by fire. It seems almost impossible to believe there is a good and loving God. But the hope in God is what truly sees you through."
—*Ann, 48*

"When I fought my depression, my pastor told me I needed to separate my depression from the truth that I am a Christian and God loves me and Jesus died for my sins. Sometimes, I would feel so depressed that I was sure I couldn't be a Christian. But this isn't true. Depression makes your mind think in a distorted way. Cling to the truth in depression. Repeat the truth in your mind all the time."
—*Jane, 52*

Lorraine

*PMS meant "Pack My Suitcase" for Lorraine's
husband. It was a hideous scene every
"time of the month" until Lorraine learned
practical and spiritual tips that helped her cope.*

Rolling over to hit the snooze button, Lorraine grimaced as her breasts hit the mattress. *They feel like they are going to explode,* she thought. Keeping her eyes shut, she ignored the slight headache between her eyes and fell sound asleep again. When the snooze alarm went off the second time, Lorraine slammed her hand down on the button. *That couldn't possibly have been five more minutes!* Willing her feet to the ground, she sat on the edge of the bed rubbing her temples. "My head hurts." She nudged her husband. "I need coffee, Jack."

He only grunted in response.

Dragging herself into the kitchen, she poured water into the coffeemaker. When she glanced up, she saw a pile of dirty dishes sitting in the sink. "Ugh!" she blurted. "Who do the kids think I am?" Unable to stifle her anger, she began banging around the kitchen. "It's ridiculous," she ranted. "How many times have I told them to wash their own dishes?"

"Coffee ready?" Jack drifted into the kitchen.

"Do you see this?" Lorraine was indignant.

"What?"

"This," she said, pointing to the sink. "These kids completely take me for granted."

"Ah, come on, hon. It's just a few dishes."

His tone grated. "That's the point. A few dishes here, a dirty sock there, and before you know it, I'm Miss Merry Maid." Her voice was loud and shrill.

Knowing better than to engage, Jack quietly retreated back to the bedroom with his mug of coffee.

Raking her fingers through her hair, Lorraine realized she was over-reacting. *What is my problem?* She stared blankly at the sink. Rubbing her temples again, she walked over to the magnetic calendar sticking to the fridge. When she saw the date she groaned. "Oh great. Here we go again. It's PMS."

She dragged into the bathroom and undressed to take a shower. Her eyes blazed as they fixated on Jack's clothes piled in the corner. She clenched her teeth as foul thoughts bombarded her mind. *He never does anything I ask. Never! How tough is it for a grown man to pick up his clothes? Didn't his mother ever teach him to pick up after himself?* As she stepped into the shower the high-pressure water came crashing down on her sore breasts. "Ouch!" she howled. She stood on her tiptoes, try-ing to lessen the pressure, but that only made it worse. "This is not working!" she screamed.

"Here, honey, I'll do it." Jack quickly came in and adjusted the knob. "Hey, you okay?"

"No I'm not." She dropped the shampoo on her foot and screamed again.

"Anything I can do to help?"

She looked at Jack, deciding whether to yell at him or cry. *He is being so nice. I can't yell at him.* So she started crying. Shampoo ran into her eyes, causing her to cry harder. "I feel totally out of control every month when this happens," she whimpered.

"Honey, I have been married to you for 20 years. This isn't the real you."

"So? Right now I hate myself."

"Just do what you need to do today to take care of yourself. And don't worry about dinner tonight. I'll take the kids out."

He was being too nice again. Tears kept spilling down her cheeks. "I don't deserve you," she croaked.

"Come on. Rinse your hair and I'll get you a towel."

Like an obedient child, Lorraine rinsed out the shampoo and stepped onto the floor mat. She tugged on her ugliest sweats and went to the kitchen to make lunches for the kids.

"Mom, did you sign the field trip release form?" Amanda asked, slurping down a bowl of cereal.

"What are you talking about? You never gave me a release form!" she snapped.

"Yeah I did, Mom. Last night."

"Amanda, I obviously would have remembered if you gave it to me."

"But, I—"

"Stop talking back." Lorraine could feel herself losing it. She knew she was being irrational but she launched ahead anyway. "I've had it with your back talk. Forget about the form. You're late. HURRY!"

As Amanda walked out of the room, Lorraine could see the hurt in her daughter's eyes. Guilt gripped her. *I'm the world's worst mother.* She sat down and held her head between her hands.

After getting her three kids off to school, Lorraine picked up the phone and began canceling. "Suz? Hey, it's me. I'm sorry I can't do lunch today. I just need to lay low."

"PMS?"

"Yeah. I've cried twice already, had hateful thoughts about everyone I live with, and attacked the showerhead."

"Just think. It's only nine o'clock," Suzie chuckled.

"Off to a great start, aren't I?"

"Sweetie, we have been friends long enough for you to know I understand about lunch. But listen. When Satan tries to convince you that you add no value to the human race, you rebuke him. He's the Father of Lies. Do you hear me?"

"Yeah. I'll try." She felt encouraged that her friend knew her so well.

"Okay. I'll be praying for you today."

"Thanks."

Next she dialed her writing partner. "Nancy, can we reschedule the conference call? I am not thinking well today."

"PMS?"

"Of course. What else?"

"I could tell the minute I heard your voice. You always sound a little different. Is it really bad this month?"

"I can't tell yet. But I don't think so." Lorraine tried the power of positive thinking approach.

Hanging up the phone, she walked into the office and picked up her prayer journal. She sat at her desk for a long time trying to think but her mind felt foggy. She frowned. Yesterday's journal entry was filled with praise and gratitude. *How could I have possibly felt that way 24 hours ago? I've obviously had a complete identity change.* Picking up the pen, she started to write.

> *"During my PMS, I find myself apologizing a lot."—Lorraine, 50*
>
> ⁀

God, how I despise my flesh. In it dwells no good thing. I hate the critical thoughts, the utter selfishness, and the inability to get beyond me. I want it dead. Some friends are coming over tonight for Bible study on the book The Practice of the Presence of God. *I feel anything but holy right now. I want to call them and tell them not to come. My flesh has taken over. I just want to sit here and cry and whine and complain.*

She slammed her journal shut and flung down her pen. She didn't feel any better.

I need to run, she thought. *I need to sweat.* She changed into her running clothes and took off down the dirt road of her neighborhood.

She wanted to quit during the first mile. But when the endorphins kicked in and sweat began dripping down her forehead, she didn't want to stop. Pounding the dirt road, she felt the out-of-control emotions settle down as she ran faster and longer. Finally, when her legs felt like noodles, she turned around and headed home. Reaching the front porch, she collapsed into the white wicker rocker, her body glistening with sweat. "Okay," she said, looking up at the clear blue sky. "Now I feel a little better."

Convinced she might actually be able to accomplish something for the day, she walked inside, mulling over which project on her desk was most pressing. Filling up a large glass with water, she began craving sweets. "Stay away from chocolate," warned the PMS seminar experts. "It has caffeine." *I don't care what those stupid PMS experts preach. I need chocolate. Now!* Rummaging through the snack drawer for the bag of Hershey's Kisses, she became incensed. "Did they eat them all?" Panic rose and she began rummaging through every kitchen cupboard. Coming up empty-handed, she sunk to the linoleum floor as loud gut-wrenching sobs took over.

After a long cry she blotted her eyes dry with a dirty dishtowel and slowly stood. All she longed to do was find the darkest corner in the house and curl up underneath a blanket. *No, Lorraine,* she berated herself. *You've done that before and Satan always takes over until you absolutely despise yourself. Do something that helps. Like a bubble bath and a good, sad book to make you cry some more. That will help—maybe.*

When Jack got home late that afternoon and found Lorraine in bed, her puffy eyes told her story. "Didn't go so well today, huh?" He sat down and began rubbing her feet.

"Who am I to be in ministry? What good am I to anyone?" she croaked over fresh tears. "I'm a wreck."

"Hon, you know this only lasts a couple more days and then you'll be yourself again out there conquering the world."

"Yeah, maybe," she said, her head hanging down.

She hunkered down in bed the rest of the evening, and before she slipped into sleep, she stated with authority, "Get behind me, Satan. I refuse to let you have victory. I do not believe your lies. Lord, help me close the door to any stronghold for Satan tomorrow. Help me have a better day."

That night when Jack and the kids returned from dinner, he opened the bedroom door and saw Lorraine curled up on her side. Lorraine kept quiet, hoping he would think she was asleep.

"It's only 8:30, Dad. Why is Mom in bed already?" asked Jonathon.

"She's not feeling well. Now come on, let's get your homework done."

True to Jack's prediction, in a couple of days, the PMS black shroud lifted, revealing the real Lorraine. That morning when her alarm clock went off, she was wide awake, ready to seize the day with her normal positive energy. Before climbing out of bed she wrapped her arms around sleeping Jack. *I love him so much*, she thought, pecking him on the cheek. With the coffee brewing, she sat down at the kitchen table and opened her prayer journal. Her heart bursting with thanksgiving, she wrote a new day's entry.

> *"Give yourself grace when you're having PMS."*
> *—Lorraine*

God, You are so magnificent. You are so wonderful. Thank You for what You showed me in Your Word this morning. Thank You for changing me. Thank You.

When Jack walked into the kitchen, he took one look at his wife. "Feeling good?" he asked with a smile.

She laughed. "Yep. Thank God. I'm back."

Today, after dealing with debilitating PMS every month for more than 20 years, Lorraine has learned a lot about the monthly syndrome that plagues so many women. "There are over 300 symptoms of PMS and I have almost every one of them," she explains. "And for me, like so many other women, it has gotten worse as I have gotten older. I knew it wasn't going away until menopause so I needed to figure out a better way to deal with it than just blowing up like a volcano every month."

Here are a few tricks that help her manage the battle better:
• Get more sleep when you have PMS.
• Sweat as much as you can to release the toxins.
• Don't talk about finances or anything else important with your husband when you have PMS.
• Tell your close friends so they know what to expect from you every month.
• When you feel overcome by anger, shut your mouth, breathe deeply, and walk away.
• Understand your limitations. Cut at least half off your schedule during PMS.
• Take care of yourself. Take a bubble bath and lay low as much as you can.
• Crying frequently also releases the toxins. Watch a sad movie or read a sad book.
• If you crave chocolate—EAT IT!

"Women with bad PMS need to understand they are physically, mentally, and emotionally limited during those days of the month. But the most important thing for a Christian woman to understand is that PMS can be an opening for Satan to undermine her identity and discredit her."

Lorraine knows this firsthand because during her PMS, she found herself believing she was worthless and terrible at everything she did. It was so extreme that there were times she felt suicidal.

Once she really understood how vulnerable she was to Satan's stream of lies, she could fight back using Scripture and prayer. "The more I learned what was happening to me during PMS, the more I understood I really needed to alter my lifestyle during those few days a month." She now assesses each month to see how the PMS is and makes a choice of what to keep in and what to take out of her schedule.

"And usually I cut everything I can so my husband won't pack his suitcase," Lorraine smiles.

In Their Footsteps

"I have learned to work with my body instead of fight it. I used to ignore my PMS. Now, I recognize it and listen to my body and what it needs."
—*Amy, 52*

"When I feel like killing my husband, I know it is my hormones taking over and I have learned to retreat and not engage in arguments."
—*Jillian, 50*

"You need to get support from your friends. Lots of times, even girl-friends can't relate but it is important to open up with a few close friends. It will help them understand you better and they can be praying for you."
—*Lisa, 50*

"Mark your PMS days on your calendar and put off stressful situations. Also, gather all the health information you can and then spend time with the Lord."
—*Thais, 42*

"Focus on the light of God's love in the midst of the darkness of your depression and walk toward that light."
—*Linette, 52*

Depression Summary

ᏇᎧ

Are you having trouble sleeping or eating well? Are you crying more than usual? Is it difficult for you to get out of bed each morning? Are you feeling low on energy? Do you think you might be depressed but you don't think anyone will understand? You are not alone! Some seven million women in the United States have clinical depression, but there is hope.

The women in this chapter all battled the blues and won. Whether depression is caused by an event like abuse, as in Amy's case, or from hormonal imbalance, such as Lorraine, or from an inherited propensity for depression, there is hope for defeating this debilitating disease. Both of these women are living examples of overcoming depression. So don't despair, but do seek help.

Mark the following factors that exist in your own life:

_____ Chronic stress like ongoing financial or marital problems.

_____ A stressful event like a move, job loss, or divorce.

_____ An intangible loss like the loss of a dream, hope, purpose, or identity.

_____ Taking on more than you can handle.

_____ Suffering from a physical illness or disability.

_____ Unresolved negative emotions like anger, grief, bitterness, envy, shame, etc.

_____ A tangible loss, such as losing a friend, relative, home, or income.

_____ Unrealistic expectations of others or of yourself.

_____ Premenstrual mood swings.

One or any combination of these factors can contribute to depression. What steps can you take to eliminate or better handle these factors?

Do you have someone in your life you can talk to about your feelings?

Do you know someone who you think might be depressed? What do you think you can do to help them?

Suggestions:

1. Seek help today! If you think you might be suffering from depression, call your doctor *and* your pastor. Find an older woman to walk with you through your depression.
2. Pray for God to comfort you in a special, personal way. Seek your own mental picture of Jesus loving and comforting you.
3. Read the Psalms each day.
4. If you have a friend who is depressed, let that person know you care about her. Ask her how she's doing, and invite her to do something simple like take a walk together. Or if you have a friend who suffers from PMS, give her a gift to lift her spirits during her downtime.

chapter eight

where women walked . . .

through abuse

Pauline

Pauline's life was filled with physical and verbal abuse, yet she allowed the pain from her abuse to be molded into a deep compassion for other hurting people.

Pauline clutched her knees to her chest, trying to make her scrawny 11-year-old body as small as possible. *God, please don't let the mice or spiders get me,* she prayed, hugging herself tighter as she crouched on the pitch-black stairwell. Her stomach grumbled, but she felt numb to the hunger pains after not eating for three days. She heard a noise at the bottom of the stairway, and her whole body shuddered. Worse than being beaten or locked in the cellar were the creepy-crawly creatures that lurked below her on the cold cement floor.

God, I'm sorry I'm a bad girl, Pauline prayed, trying to ignore the little scurrying sounds she heard below her. Her mind felt foggy as she tried to remember what she had done to make her mom and dad mad this time. *Was it the dish I broke? I'm sorry. I'll be more careful. I promise. Please make them let me out of here.* She tried to pray some more but slipped into a fitful sleep. When the cellar doors opened, the glaring light stung her eyes even before she opened them.

"Get up," ordered her mother. "You have work to do."

Pauline put her hands against the wall to steady herself and then pushed herself up. Her legs felt wobbly and a wave of dizziness swept over her. For the next two hours she brought in the firewood, fed the animals and cleaned their hutches, swept the floor, and did some wash. When her mom left the house for an errand, Pauline walked over to the kitchen table where her sister was coloring a picture and sat down. She felt an intense urge all of a sudden to draw a picture. Forgetting the work she still had left to do, she picked up a pencil and began to sketch.

"What are you drawing?" asked her sister, watching Pauline.

Pauline shrugged. "I don't know." She made swift strokes with her pencil. She had always loved to draw but at that moment, she felt more than just *wanting* to draw—she *had* to draw.

"It's a man," commented her sister as Pauline continued to fill in the picture.

When Pauline finished, she set down her pencil and looked at the picture she'd drawn. *It's Jesus,* she thought, stupefied at her own work.

She'd only recently seen Jesus when her father started taking her to church. The first Sunday when she entered the sanctuary, she saw a crucifix with this man hanging upon it. She had stared, unbelieving. *He reminds me of the man who sits with me on the stairs when I'm locked in the cellar,* she thought while her eyes drank in His face. *You are God, aren't You?* she whispered. From then on Pauline knew who to pray to. When she felt scared, she would curl up on her bed with the picture she had drawn and pray. *Dear God, help me be a good girl. Don't let my parents hurt me anymore.*

That day, as she sat looking at her drawing, she felt the same peace that Jesus always gave her in the basement.

Before continuing her chores, Pauline stashed the picture in a safe place in her bedroom. That night Pauline's mother did not allow her to eat dinner with the family. "You're ugly and dumb. Go upstairs and I'll tell you when you can come down."

Her mother's words rang in her head as she lay on her bed in her room alone. The smell of the food made her stomach burn. Finally, the hunger pangs were too intense for her to just lie there so she got up and tiptoed into the bathroom and looked at her reflection in the mirror. *I'm so ugly,* she thought with tears glistening in her eyes. She looked so different from her sister and second oldest brother. They both had light hair and light eyes. She glared at her dark brown eyes and long, dark, braided hair. *Why can't I look like them?* Tears rolled down her cheeks as she thought about her oldest brother. *I look like him. But why doesn't Mom hate him as much as me?* Staring at herself, she undid her thick braids and began to redo them. As she wove her hair into fresh braids, another thought struck her and more tears flowed. *It's because I'm stupid. They hate me because I never do anything right.* Suddenly, her mother's shrill voice pierced the air. "Pauline! Get down here!"

> *"No matter what happened to me, I always believed in God and I always prayed."*
> —*Pauline, 64*

Her heart started pounding as she quickly dried her eyes. She flung the bathroom door open and hurried down the stairs.

"Yes." Pauline's voice was just above a whisper.

Her mother pointed to the sink. "Clean up."

Obediently, Pauline walked over to the sink and filled it with hot soapy water. She cleared the dishes from the table and devoured the leftovers before she scrubbed the plates. That night before she went to bed, she took out the picture she had made earlier that day. She fell asleep with the picture resting on her chest.

Several years later when Pauline was 17, she met Thomas, a young man who brazenly flirted with her at every opportunity.

Pauline didn't care. "I don't want to go out with him, Mom," she said when she found out Thomas had asked permission to take her out.

"Why not? No one else is going to want you," her mother spat with a curled lip. "You're too ugly."

Still, her mother wouldn't give him permission unless he helped with some house projects she wanted done.

Reluctantly, Pauline went on a date with Thomas. He continued to pursue her and after several months of dating, she agreed to marry him, telling herself it would be better than living at home. But Thomas treated her just like her parents had treated her. He beat her, cheated on her, and told her she was no good. Pauline accepted his abuse because deep down, she believed his words. *I am dumb. I am no good.*

Pauline got pregnant a year after they were married and Thomas was furious. "You shouldn't have let this happen. You're so stupid!" he screamed, slamming his fist into the door. Protectively, Pauline put her hands over her stomach. She wanted to run out of the room, but she knew that would infuriate him. She slunk into the corner and watched him rant and rave, throwing things around the room. Silently, she prayed he wouldn't hit her or the baby now growing inside her.

During the first six years of their marriage, they had three children. When Thomas learned about each pregnancy, he was furious. But Pauline relished being a mom. She loved nurturing her children and never once struck them as her mother had so often struck her.

Although her children brought her deep joy, life with Thomas continued to be tormented. Twelve years into the marriage, Debbie, a co-worker of Pauline's, noticed one afternoon that Pauline seemed very troubled about having to meet with a male co-worker to review some work. Pauline ended up confiding in Debbie. "My husband won't allow me to talk to another man. How can I do my job?" Pauline couldn't stop the tears as she told Debbie about her home life with Thomas.

"You don't have to live like this. It's wrong." Debbie's eyes flashed.

"But—" Pauline couldn't talk as the sobs convulsed her body. She felt afraid. She didn't know what to do.

"Marriage isn't supposed to be like this." Debbie put both her hands on Pauline's shoulders. "Pauline, you should never accept being physically abused. You have to do something about this." Pauline wiped her nose with a tissue and looked at Debbie. She saw compassion in her eyes. *She's right*, thought Pauline. *She's right.*

Debbie helped Pauline find a counseling center close to work so

Pauline could meet with a counselor during her lunch hour. Over the next seven years, Pauline went to counseling, and her confidence and self-worth blossomed. "You're a smart person, Pauline," her counselor told her.

"I did just get a raise at work," Pauline said, looking out the window.

At every session, her counselor encouraged her. Gradually she began to see the lies that she lived with. Lies she'd always believed were truth. She saw that the way Thomas treated her was wrong and she came to the point where she knew she had to make a change in her life.

"Thomas, please come talk to my counselor with me," Pauline pleaded one night. "We need to get help for our marriage."

"What for? I don't need anyone to tell me anything. You have the problem, so you go talk to her."

"But . . . "

Thomas turned up the volume of the television, drowning out Pauline's voice.

She tried repeatedly to get Thomas to listen to her and change his behavior, but he dismissed anything she had to say. He also continued seeing other women and abusing her when he drank too much. It took her three tries, but finally Pauline left Thomas.

In spite of her harrowing life of abuse, Pauline's heart was filled with love and compassion, and she yearned to help others in need—others like herself. She began to volunteer at the city hospital with abused babies. Every afternoon after work, Pauline would drive to the hospital to help take care of little babies.

"Thank God you're here," a nurse said one afternoon as Pauline wrote her name on the volunteer sign-in sheet. "It's been one of those days. We can't make any of them happy."

Pauline walked into the nursery and picked up the first crying baby she came to. She changed his diaper, warmed a bottle, fed him, and then sat in a chair with him cradled in her arms and rocked back and forth. After he fell sound asleep, she swaddled him in a blanket and set him down in his crib. She walked over to the next bassinet and picked up another crying baby. She changed her, fed her, cradled and rocked her, and set the peaceful baby back into her bassinet. She went through the whole nursery and, one by one, calmed each baby.

"It seems like every baby you hold stops crying," said a new nurse working in the nursery with Pauline that evening.

Pauline smiled down at the dark-haired little baby she was holding. She stroked his wispy tuft of black hair. Her throat tightened as she looked at him. *How could someone hurt him,* she thought. *He's so perfect. So innocent.* She clutched him close to her chest and squeezed her eyes shut. *Please, God, protect this little child.*

After four years of volunteering with babies, Pauline felt that it was time for her to move on. She had grown too attached to some of the children, and it was torture saying good-bye to so many babies she loved. She began volunteering at a counseling center for troubled teens. One evening she was leading a group session. She shared how her own son had been taking drugs but, through a teen counseling program, decided to quit and make better choices for his life. Arturo, a 14-year-old boy in her group, slouched down in his chair and glared at her the whole time she talked.

After the session Pauline walked out to her car. It was snowing, so she hurried through the dark parking lot. Out of the corner of her eye, she saw Arturo following her. *Oh no. What's he going to do to me?* She fumbled quickly through her purse and with shaky hands stuck her key into the door lock.

"Hey, lady." Arturo's voice spewed hostility.

"Yes?" Pauline turned around trying to act calm.

"What you said in there—you're full of it! That story about your son ain't true. You're just a wanna-be white woman who's rich and comes over here and tells cute little stories. But you don't know nothin' about our kind of life."

Pauline shook her head. "Everything I said in there was true. And I'm not rich. I'm barely making it. I work all day and come over here and volunteer at night."

He scowled at her.

"Arturo," she spoke in a soft voice. "I bet I know more about your life than you would believe. I just want to help."

"Yeah, right. Well then let me ask you a question, lady. You want to help? Will you give me a ride home?"

"Sure," answered Pauline before thinking. As he climbed into the car, she turned on the ignition with trembling hands and then gripped the steering wheel trying to steady herself. "Where am I going?" she asked, attempting to appear casual.

"I'll tell you when to turn," he grunted.

As Pauline drove farther and farther, she realized he lived in one of the most dangerous neighborhoods in the city. When Arturo pointed down a dark street, she hesitated for a moment, then made herself turn the steering wheel. As she drove down the street, she saw a large gang of boys appear from behind trees and houses and trash cans. *Oh, God. They are going to rape and murder me,* she thought with trepidation. Arturo pointed to a beaten-down house. Not knowing what else to do, Pauline stopped the car in front of the house.

"You say you know about my life. What do you know?" His eyes were dark as he challenged her.

"Have you ever been beaten by your mother with a stick?" asked Pauline.

"Yeah, sure." He rolled his eyes.

"Well, I was in the hospital for two weeks and had to lie on my stomach the whole time because my mom beat me so badly on my back and legs."

"So. That's nothing."

"Have you ever had your hands put in boiling water?"

"No." He still didn't appear impressed.

"Well, my mom dunked my hands in a pot of boiling water and the doctors had to take skin from my bottom and graft it onto my hands." She held up her hand to show him, but it was too dark to see them.

He shrugged.

"One time, my husband put a fork through my hand."

"Really? My dad did that to my mom too." His interest was piqued.

They continued to talk for a long time. And then, while Pauline was in the middle of sharing another story, Arturo began crying. Pauline reached over and hugged him, letting him cry on her shoulder. "You *are* one of us," he choked through his tears.

Pauline's heart broke for him and tears began to stream down her face as she embraced him. Looking up at her, Arturo whispered, "I've never had an adult hug me before."

After a long moment he wiped his eyes and, without warning, opened the car door and stuck his hand up in the air, giving some sort of signal. Pauline looked around as the gang disappeared.

"What did you do?" she asked in amazement.

"I told them you were cool. And now they know your car so if you're ever in trouble, you come here and my boys will take care of you." He smiled at her for the first time.

They talked a little more and then said good night. "See you tomorrow at the center," Pauline said to him as he got out of the car.

Driving home, Pauline felt a sense of accomplishment. *I think I might have gotten through. Just a little. Help him, God.*

The next night Pauline joked around with Arturo and told him he needed to get some exercise. "Look at you. You're too pale."

"Oh yeah. When do you exercise?" He still spoke with an attitude.

"I walk several times a week during my lunch break. You could come with me."

He scoffed and walked away.

After the group session that evening Arturo found a moment when Pauline was alone. "So uh, where uh, when did you say you walked?"

Pauline smiled at him and they made plans to meet later in the week for a walk at a big city park near her work. "But don't wear those clothes." She pointed at him. "Not that big baggy stuff, and no gang colors or earrings either."

A few days later Pauline arrived at their designated meeting spot but didn't see Arturo anywhere.

"Hey, lady," she heard Arturo's voice behind her. She turned around and broke into a big smile. There he stood in straight-legged jeans, a T-shirt, and tennis shoes.

"Hey, you look great!"

His face flushed and he looked down.

Pauline continued to befriend Arturo and started teaching him how to read. They met every day during the summer and within three months, Arturo could read sixth-grade-level books. He beamed every time he finished a book and Pauline's heart swelled with love for him. Arturo started affectionately calling her "Mom." She continued to encourage him, telling him that he had a promising future and that he didn't need the gang.

One afternoon Pauline waited in the library for Arturo but he didn't show up. She looked at her watch and after 45 minutes gave up and went home. When she walked into her apartment she saw the red light flashing on her answering machine. She pushed the PLAY button and her heart skipped when she heard Arturo's nervous voice.

"Mom. Something bad's going down and I have to get out of here. I'll call you when I can."

Click.

Pauline sank down on the floor. *God, protect him. Don't let anything happen to him.* She kept praying every day for several months and then one evening, her phone rang. When she answered it and heard his voice, her heart leaped.

"Mom, I'm okay."

"Where are you? What happened?" She collapsed into a kitchen chair, her whole body feeling a wave of relief.

"I made a mistake. I told one of the gang boys I was learning to read. He pretended he was interested and asked me lots of questions. Then he finked on me. He was going to our leader and I knew what that meant. I had to get out."

They talked for 20 minutes and Arturo told Pauline he was with his sister in California. He said he had plans to get his GED and go to college.

When she hung up, Pauline sat smiling in the kitchen for a long time. *Thank You, God.*

She received a letter from Arturo a few months later. Her eyes welled up with tears as she read it. Not one word was misspelled and the penmanship was beautiful. He sent a picture of himself too. She couldn't believe how clean-cut he looked with short hair. "Look, Mom," he wrote on the back of the picture. "Check it out. Looking good, huh?"

Today Pauline continues to have a heart for children who come from abusive homes. She channels the memories she has from her own hideous childhood into a deep concern and compassion for others. Although she has forgiven her mother for all the abuse she inflicted on Pauline, scars from her abuse—both physical and emotional—still remain. For instance, she still has a hard time believing she is beautiful. The harsh words of her mother continue to resonate in her mind. But she is beautiful. She has prominent cheekbones and her soft, light-brown skin glows, making her look 10 years younger than she is. Her warm eyes sparkle and her brilliant smile amplifies her beauty.

> *"I finally have come to believe I am not dumb. I know I am smart. I know those were lies that I was told and believed as a child and even as an adult."—Pauline*

ᏬᏇ

Her beauty on the inside is even more profound. She made a choice throughout her abuse to cling to God even before she was formally taught about Him. And many years after she drew the picture of Christ she learned all about Jesus and committed her life to Him.

Pauline's story is a true story of victory. Instead of being crushed by her abuse and abusers, she has allowed her experiences to be a point of ministry to others.

In Their Footsteps

"People who have been physically abused have had something taken from them. I believe that God is the only true Healer for them, but sometimes they need professional people to help them work through all they have lost and allow God's healing to take place."
—*Joyce, 59*

"It is important to get out of your own circumstances and help others. Even though you actually may be doing something for someone else, you receive the blessing."
—*Doris, 62*

"It is amazing the healing God can do with an open heart. He is the only one who can transform a heart."
—*Linda, 55*

Karen

Karen's son was sexually victimized by a man whom many families in their community trusted. Through her painful journey Karen learned that no matter how deep the pain, in Christ we don't have to live defeated by our circumstances.

Karen stood at the kitchen sink chopping onions for dinner when someone pounded loudly on the front door. "Mark, can you get the door?" she called out to her 13-year-old son.

She heard the front door open and a deep voice talking. After rinsing her hands, Karen whisked out of the kitchen to greet their unexpected visitor. Standing in the doorway was Raymond Fitzpatrick, a friend of theirs from church who was a police detective. He towered over Mark and looked intimidating in his official police uniform. "Hey," Karen smiled at him. "What's going on?"

"How are you, Karen?" Raymond's voice seemed tense and Karen looked at him, puzzled. "We're in the neighborhood going around to different houses and talking to kids involved with Mr. Thomas in the Kids Night Out program."

"Oh sure," Karen nodded her head and looked at her son. Mark dropped his gaze the moment she looked at him.

"If you don't mind," Raymond cleared his throat, "I'll just talk to Mark alone for a few minutes."

"Of course." Karen felt an uncomfortable churning in the pit of her stomach. "Do you want to sit out on the porch?" she asked, gesturing out the window toward two patio chairs.

Detective Fitzpatrick opened the front door and Mark turned to go outside. Karen stood frozen for a moment, watching them. Walking back into the kitchen, she paced back and forth. *Of course nothing happened,* she thought, rubbing her forehead with both hands. *That would be impossible. I know everything that goes on with my children.*

But something deep inside her felt afraid.

For the past six months Mark had worked for Mr. Thomas at the local recreation center, helping facilitate games and activities for local youth. The previous week one of the boys on his team had told his parents and the police that Mr. Thomas had sexually abused him. Karen and Doug, her husband, had been watching the story unfold in the local news. When they had asked Mark about it, he just shrugged it off and didn't have much to say. But that was nothing new. Lately he had been the infamous moody teenager and didn't have much to say about anything, especially to his mom and dad.

Karen heard the porch door squeak open and quickly darted back to the entryway. "Thanks, Mark," the detective said as he tilted his head and gestured to Karen to come outside with him. Her heart raced as she followed him to the porch. "Karen, I want you to know that Mark told us nothing happened to him. But we think this guy has victimized a lot more kids than just the one boy. So please keep your eyes and ears open for anything unusual."

Relief swept over Karen. *Thank God,* she thought, letting out a deep breath. "I will." As he turned to walk away, Karen called after him, "Please let us know if you find out anything more."

Karen walked back into the house and leaned against the door as she closed it. *Those poor parents. I don't know what I would do if anything like that ever happened to one of my kids.* She closed her eyes and shuddered at the thought. She felt comforted by the fact that she had always been an attentive mother, knowing exactly where her children were, whom they were with, and what they were doing. As she walked back into the house she glanced up the stairs and saw Mark's door closed. She again whispered a prayer of thanksgiving for Mark's safety but as she finished preparing dinner, her heart grieved for the mother of the other boy who had been victimized.

The next afternoon she was throwing a load of laundry into the washing machine when the phone rang. She answered on the first ring. "Hello?"

"Mrs. Campbell?"

"Yes?" She didn't recognize the voice.

"This is Officer Cain at the Broomston Police Department, and we are calling to let you know we have Mark down here. He and a friend came in about a half hour ago to let us know that Mr. Thomas sexually victimized them, too."

Karen gasped. A siren went off in her head. *No! Not my Mark! Oh, God, don't let it be true. Please . . .*

"Can you come down to the station?" The policeman's voice sounded like it was coming down a long tunnel.

Her mind felt thick with confusion. Nodding her head she whimpered, "Yes," and hung up the phone.

Her hand trembled as she dialed her husband's work phone number. She couldn't reach him. Numbly she picked up her keys and walked to her car. When she arrived at the police station, two officers ushered her into an empty room. Before she saw Mark, they explained to her what would happen next. When they told her Mark would have to testify against Mr. Thomas, her head started reeling all over again. She couldn't concentrate on what they were saying. *Please*

> *"Sex repulsed me for a long time. My husband and I had to work through that together. He felt as sick as I did."*—Karen, 45

no. Not my baby. Nausea swept over her and she excused herself to the bathroom. Leaning over the toilet, her whole body heaved with sobs. *My little boy.* She couldn't stop crying.

That night she didn't sleep. Images of what this man had done to her child kept flashing through her mind. Her thoughts couldn't break away from the question *How did this happen?* Mr. Thomas had been such a good friend to Mark and the other boys who worked with him. He had been so caring and interested in their lives. He was a well-respected youth worker in their community and even volunteered at his church with their youth group. But as Karen stared up at the dark ceiling, more pieces of the puzzle started coming together. She recalled one time when she went to pick up Mark at the recreation center and waited for him a long time out in front of the building. Finally, she walked inside and asked at the front desk if anyone knew where he was, but no one did. When she went up and knocked on Mr. Thomas's office door, she heard commotion inside and when the door opened, there were at least a dozen boys crowded around his computer looking at something. At the time she thought it was a little unusual but dismissed it. She also thought about all the showers Mark had been taking lately and the angry music he had recently started listening to. She had considered his behavior to be part of puberty, but now her stomach lurched as she realized her child had been acting out of hurt and betrayal.

A couple of days later the police called to let Karen's family know that Mr. Thomas had fled the area. Police searched for a week and then found him dead in his truck. He had committed suicide. Even though Karen felt enraged and devastated by what Mr. Thomas had done to her son, the man's tragic death only left their family with more agony. Mark struggled with thinking he was at fault for Mr. Thomas's death. And should Mark go to his funeral? Mr. Thomas had been his friend, hadn't he? It was all so confusing.

Karen and her husband, Brian, did anything they could to help their son walk through such painful circumstances. They continually let him know that he had no reason to feel shame, and they made sure never to impose any feeling of blame on him with "why?" questions. They also arranged for their youth pastor, Greg, from church to meet with Mark on a weekly basis. Every week Greg would take Mark out for soda or ice cream and just be with him and listen to him. Mark could tell Greg things he did not feel comfortable talking about with his mom and dad. They met together for over a year and their relationship was instrumental in Mark's healing process.

> *"God was such a gentleman with me through this whole journey. As He walked with me through all my sorrow He gently pointed out my own weaknesses and faults. He wanted me to grow through all of this."*
> —*Karen*

ᏝᏝ

Karen's healing took a long time too. For months she spent the better part of each day praying and reading her Bible. Each morning after getting her kids off to school, she turned on a worship tape and sat down at the kitchen table with her journal. One morning when she felt particularly alone in her pain, she wrote with tears dripping down, smearing the black ink. *Lord, I can't go to any of my friends. I need to guard and protect Mark right now. He has been hurt too much and I don't want to take any chances that friends at church would look at him differently. Lord, be with me. You're all I have to cling to in this dark hour.*

She couldn't write any more so she set the pen down and closed her eyes. The praise music slowly seeped into her heart, wrapping around her spirit with penetrating warmth. She felt God crying alongside her. *My heart breaks too,* she heard Him whisper. *But remember I am also the God who will take care of every injustice in this world.*

Karen felt an intimacy with God she had never had before. Gradually, she felt the pieces of her broken heart be put back together. One weekend several years later, she went away with her sisters to work on putting together their photo albums. Laughing and talking, Karen and her sisters cut and pasted pictures into colorful, creative albums. As Karen flipped through a pile of pictures she stopped abruptly when she came to a photo of Mark when he was six years old. He had a buzz hair-cut and sported a blue T-shirt and beat-up sneakers. His head was tipped slightly and on his face he wore his trademark thin-lipped, imp-ish grin. As Karen stared at the picture the old pain came welling up, and her eyes glistened with tears.

"What's wrong?" her younger sister asked reaching out to hold Karen's hand.

Words stuck in her throat as she held on to the picture and cried. Finally in a soft voice she said, "That's the one thing you can never have back. He had such an innocence about him." Her voice broke off and tears rolled down her cheeks. "And that man stole it," she whispered.

The pain of Mark's victimization still pierces Karen's heart every time she looks at that photo—but she is grateful beyond words for how well Mark is doing now as a young adult. He has his own deep relationship with Christ and feels called into youth ministry.

A hard lesson Karen learned through their tribulation was that not only did Mark need support,

> *"God showed me that He wishes this didn't hap-pened as much as I did. But He will take care of all injustices in the end."—Karen*

∾

prayer, and extra love during this time but his twin brother needed it too. Karen and her husband were so fixated on helping Mark that they overlooked the needs of Aaron. As a result, Aaron began harboring a deep hatred for the man who had hurt his brother. Looking back, Karen wishes she had been sensitive to the pain Aaron experienced as well.

In their journey, Karen experienced God's tender comfort in a pro-found way. She also felt the promise of His justice, which freed her from being consumed with bitterness and vengeance. And she now lives with an empowering spiritual lesson alive in her heart: "As Chris-tians, we have victory to overcome the sin that happens to us and not be defeated by our circumstances."

In Their Footsteps

"The hardest thing in the world is to see one of your children get hurt. Instead of getting angry with God whenever one of my children would get hurt, I always went to God and asked for His help. It felt freeing."
—*Betsy, 63*

"It is important to remember we live in a fallen world where there are bad people who do bad things. God will rule over eternity but Satan rules the earth."
—*Diane, 55*

"I spent many hours on my knees praying for my kids. I believe God listens to a mother's prayers."
—*Cindy, 52*

"Jesus never promised that everything would be as you dreamed when you were younger and before you were knocked about by life's circumstances. However, He does promise He will be with you through all of life's joys and sorrows."
—*Lori, 50*

Andrea

*After surviving an abusive childhood, Andrea is learning
to live the abundant life God wants her to live.*

Andrea carefully slipped her tiny fingers, one by one, into her new bright white gloves. She stepped onto the little stool in the bathroom, stood on her tippy-toes, and took a good look at herself. *Perfect! I look like a princess,* she thought as she admired herself from head to toe. She wore a little white satin dress, new white lace socks, stiff white patent leather shoes, a white bonnet, a white purse, and the spotless white gloves. *I wonder if Daddy will think I look pretty.*

She could hear the television in the living room and knew her daddy would be lying on the couch watching it. That's what he always did. So she grabbed her purse and ventured out to show off her new Easter outfit. As she passed her seven-year-old brother, Daniel, he smirked, "What's up, freckle face?"

"How do I look, Danny?" she asked, ignoring his comment. Today, nothing anyone said would make her feel bad.

"You look like Casper the ghost with freckles," he laughed.

"I don't care what you think. I think I look beautiful," she retorted and pranced into the living room to model her new dress for her daddy.

She waltzed into the dark room, lit only by the glow of the television. Her daddy lay on the couch, just like she expected. She stood right in front of the TV. "Look at me, Daddy. Do you think I look pretty?" she asked as she twirled around once to show off her satin dress. She just loved how it looked when she spun around.

> *"Have the courage to be the first one to break the negative cycle of abuse in your family. And it does take a lot of courage."*
> —Andrea, 48

When she turned again to face her daddy, fear gripped her heart. Rage was written all over his face. He suddenly, violently tipped over the coffee table, causing books, glasses, and papers to scatter onto the floor. "Get out of the way!" he hollered as he jumped up and started toward her. "What's wrong with you? Can't you see I'm trying to watch TV? You're standing right in front of it, you worthless little . . ." His rage escalated. He began throwing furniture around the room, screaming profanities at her.

Five-year-old Andrea froze with fear. Daniel ran into the room and grabbed her by the hand. "Come on, Andy, you've got to get out of here," he said pulling her away from their dad.

He pulled her from the living room and out the kitchen door into the alley. They ran down the alley, away from the crashing and screaming coming from their home. "Daddy's really mad this time. You'd better hide," Daniel said.

They crouched down behind some big garbage cans. Andrea gathered the hem of her white satin dress and tucked it under her body to make sure she couldn't be seen. The stink of the garbage permeated the air around them. But that didn't matter. They were safe for now.

"Danny," Andrea asked when her fear calmed down and tears trickled down her little cheeks. "Why did Daddy get so mad? I just wanted to show him my new dress."

"I don't know. You know how he is. You just never know when he's gonna get mad. Just stay out of his way," Daniel advised. After what seemed like a long time to two little children, their mom drove up in the car and gruffly said, "Get in the car!"

From that moment on Andrea realized her home was not a safe place. No matter what she did or said or looked like, she couldn't make her daddy love and accept her. She believed his harsh words. She felt worthless, unlovable, and dirty—like the garbage she hid behind.

Andrea's father's rages were not rare. He exploded almost weekly. Sometimes he let loose verbally, other times with his fists. Andrea distinctly remembers another time, about two years later, when she returned home to find her mom with two broken legs in a wheelchair. She was told her mom had been in an accident. But later she learned the truth. Apparently, her mom and dad were having a fight. Her mom had cut her dad's face with a razor blade. Then, fearing for her life, she jumped out the second-story window of their house, breaking both legs.

It wasn't just her dad who had anger problems. Her mom also struggled with irrational rage. Andrea remembers one time when she and her brother were arguing incessantly. Her mom snapped. She started laughing and called to the two kids, "Andy, Danny, come into the kitchen please."

They could hear her odd giggling and wondered what she wanted. They cautiously entered the kitchen.

"Let's all sit down on the floor together," she sweetly said. They obeyed.

"Now, Andrea, I want you to hit Danny in the face," her mother demanded, still laughing. Andrea obeyed. Then she told Danny to do the same to Andrea. She forced them to hit each other again and again, harder and harder, and she laughed as she watched them cry and hurt each other.

Andrea went to bed that night and made a vow: "When I grow up I am never going to be like my mom or dad."

Fortunately, Andrea did have a few good influences in her life. A second-grade teacher noticed how withdrawn and depressed Andrea seemed. So he placed her desk next to the friendliest, most outgoing child in class—a girl named Diane. They became fast friends and stayed best friends through high school. Andrea practically lived at Diane's house. She also loved Diane's mother, Linda. She was the kind of mother Andrea wanted to be someday. Andrea slept at Diane's house every weekend. They played with dolls, built dollhouses out of milk cartons, wrote their own plays, and did all the things she never did at home. Diane's mom often had fresh-baked cookies for them, she engaged in their playtime, and she loved Andrea like a daughter.

> *"If you have a friend recovering from abuse, she needs your support. Be available to her on a consistent basis for the long term. Don't let her isolate herself and pull away."*
> —*Andrea*

After high school Andrea met and married Gene. Andrea felt confident she could be a wife and mother like Linda. But the first seven years of their marriage were disastrous. Andrea found herself struggling with feelings of rage. She had carried her anger right into her marriage. For example, one night she made spaghetti for Gene. Andrea's mother didn't teach her how to cook and the fact was, Andrea wasn't very good at it.

"Oh, good, spaghetti tonight. That's pretty hard to mess up," Gene said, halfway joking.

"Excuse me?" Andrea said.

"Oh, I was just kidding."

"What did you say?" Andrea persisted. She could feel the anger rising inside of her like a volcano about to erupt.

"I said, at least spaghetti is pretty hard to mess up."

Andrea snapped. She picked up the plate of spaghetti covered in marinara sauce and hurled it at Gene. "Here, have your plate of spaghetti!" she screamed. She missed Gene and the pasta splattered all over the wall and floor. "I do all of this for you and you don't appreciate me." She continued to verbally berate Gene then stormed out of the kitchen—ignoring the mess that lay on the floor.

Episodes like this became fairly frequent and affected their relationship for months afterward. Fortunately, Gene didn't explode in the same manner. However, their marriage began to deteriorate.

Andrea sought help. She knew from experience what it was like to live in an anger-filled home. Now, living with a husband and two children, she didn't want her home environment to be like the one she grew up in. She desperately wanted to keep her childhood vow.

The first help she found was in a relationship with Jesus Christ. From there, her healing process began. She began seeing a Christian therapist and joined a group of other women who had been abused as children. She met weekly with this group for five years. She found incredible support and strength in the bond she felt with these women. They encouraged each other to strive for the best life possible—the life God designed them to have, not one controlled by the pain of their pasts.

> *"There comes a point when you can choose to say, 'Woe is me' or 'Wow is God.'"—Andrea*

For four years Andrea didn't have any contact with her parents. She purposely took this time away from them to develop herself. She and Gene, who became a Christian shortly after Andrea, created their own family traditions. Andrea grew in her faith and worked on healing her hurts from her childhood. After four years she began to rebuild a relationship with her mom and dad. But this time she established the rules. She determined where they would meet and under what circumstances they would relate.

Another key aspect in her healing was forgiving her mom and dad for all the pain they caused her. This wasn't easy. After attending a forgiveness seminar, Andrea did what the speaker suggested. She wrote down every little thing she felt she needed to forgive her parents for. For example, for her dad she wrote down *I forgive my dad for not thinking I was pretty that Easter.* She didn't feel anything, but she willed herself to forgive him.

Eventually, she wrote her dad and told him she had been in counseling for being abused as a child. In this letter, that her therapist helped her draft, she asked her dad to come to counseling with her. Her dad agreed to come. After an intense two-hour meeting Andrea felt incredible relief. To her astonishment, he said, "I did those things to you and I am sorry."

This marked the beginning of a new relationship with him. She never thought her dad would change, but now he showed hope and interest in building a healthy relationship.

A few years later Andrea's phone rang. It was her dad. And it was the first time he had *ever* called her.

"Hi, Andrea," he started. "You know, I was just thinking about you. Actually, I think about you a lot. And I tell the guys at work about you all the time. I tell them how proud I am of you. But I don't know if I've ever told you that. I just wanted you to know that I am proud of you. And I just wanted to make sure that you really forgive me."

"Dad, I forgave you a long time ago. You need to forgive yourself," Andrea responded, still shocked that he had called her just to praise her and ask her forgiveness.

> *"I regret the wasted time, all the time I spent ignoring my issues and thinking, 'Well, this is as good as it gets.'"—Andrea*

Today Andrea works as a counselor and lives in a loving relationship with Gene, who is now the pastor of a thriving church. They raised two children and are enjoying their three precious grandchildren. Andrea says, "To live in a place of emotional and psychological dysfunction is so far from God's best for a woman. Abundant life is not living in the past. I've put my past to rest and now I'm experiencing the abundant life God wants me to live."

In Their Footsteps

"Let your needs be known to others. Be honest about how desperately you need help. Don't pull back from others; don't isolate yourself."
—*Sande, 62*

"Trust in God and pray. He'll change you, if not your circumstances."
—*Donna, 55*

"Be active in facing your trials and suffering. Have a support group surrounding you and keep a prayer sense with you at all times, knowing that God is there for you."
—*Jan, 58*

"One thing that helped me during my times of suffering was other women who had the same experience. They listened to me talk. They understood me and the feelings I felt."
—*Jo, 65*

"I regret I did not deal with the sexual abuse when I was younger. Waiting 45 years to deal with it was way too long. Experiencing the power of forgiveness was so healing, I just wish I had dealt with all that garbage a lot sooner."
—*Gail, 59*

Abuse Summary

∾

Abuse comes in many different forms including physical, sexual, verbal, and emotional. It can happen early in life or even during the last years of an older person's life. No matter when abuse occurs, it always leaves emotional scars.

It's not easy to share a journey of abuse. It's humbling and brings up painful memories. We are very grateful to the women in this chapter for so generously sharing their difficult stories with us.

Pauline's abuse is more than most people can imagine. Yet in spite of many years of both verbal and physical mistreatment, she allowed God to turn her pain into a deep compassion for other hurting people. Karen held on tightly to the promise of God's eternal justice when her son was sexually assaulted. She also clung to God in her grief, and many mornings in her quiet time, she felt Him weeping alongside her. And Andrea found, through her faith, that it is possible to live an abundant, joy-filled life after a history of abuse.

Each of these women's lives demonstrates how in Christ the impossible becomes possible. Instead of becoming bitter, hardened, and/or perpetual victims, these women turned to Christ and allowed Him to work miracles in their damaged hearts.

Have you ever experienced abuse? If so, have you ever shared it with anyone? Why or why not? Can you find someone you trust to tell?

How do you think Satan can use childhood abuse as a stronghold in a Christian's life?

When difficult things happen in your life, do you share your struggles with a friend or a mentor, or do you walk through it alone? Why?

If God is good, why does He allow bad (abuse) in this world?

Suggestions:
1. If there is some area of your life that you struggle with and do not feel the victory of Christ, try to find an older, Christian mentor and ask her to help you walk through the struggle.
2. If you have been abused, consider going to a Christian bookstore and asking for their recommended readings on abuse issues and overcoming abuse.
3. There are many types of support groups for those abused in any way. Find one and attend. If the first group you try isn't a good fit, don't give up! Try again until you find one where you can feel comfortable sharing and growing through the pain.
4. Finding someone who has been abused to share experiences with can be very helpful. Pray together several times a week—even on the phone or over e-mail.
5. Journal your disappointment, your pain, and your anger at the perpetrator and even at God.
6. Maintain a separate journal to write psalms to God.

chapter nine

where women walked . . .

through compassion

LeAnn

*Instead of ignoring a nudging in her heart, LeAnn
responded with action. Her first small act of compassion
led to an adventure that drastically changed her life
and the lives of hundreds of children.*

Summer, 1971

"Look, girls! A bake sale. Let's stop in and buy some cupcakes," LeAnn
said as she turned her car into the church parking lot.

"Yay!" both girls shouted in unison as she unbuckled them, freeing
them from their car seats. They had spent the last couple of hours driving around their small Iowa town running errands with their mom.
They definitely deserved a treat.

"Okay, hop out. We won't be long."

"Mommy, what's that sign say?" asked LeAnn's three-year-old as she
pointed at a large banner hanging above the church entry.

"It says, 'Help raise money for the orphans in Vietnam,'" answered
LeAnn. She felt a gentle tug on her heart prompting her to help the
orphans, even if it was only to give a little money.

Inside, behind a long table laden with baked goods, sat two cheerful women wearing brightly colored, flower-print dresses. Behind them

hung heart-wrenching photographs of emaciated Vietnamese orphans. The children's dark brown eyes, showing underneath their unkempt black hair, cried out to LeAnn for help. Their swollen bellies and malformed features caused an ache in the pit of her stomach.

LeAnn found some cupcakes, paid for them, and started to leave the building.

"Thanks for stopping," one of the women said to LeAnn. "Every little bit is important to these kids."

"Glad to help," LeAnn answered. She wanted to leave, but the images of the children kept her there.

"You know these children don't have a prayer if we don't get them out of Vietnam," the woman continued.

"What do you mean?" LeAnn asked.

"Well, most of them were conceived by American servicemen. They're called 'Amerasians.' In their country they are outcasts. No one wants them. So we're working to find them good families here in America. But time is running out because the Vietcong are approaching Saigon, where our orphanage is. If these children end up in the hands of the Vietcong, they will be tortured and possibly killed."

LeAnn looked again at the photographs. Horror of what might happen to these innocent children moved her to want to do more.

> *"There is a time for every purpose under heaven. Sometimes our calling and our making a difference are to be done in the home. Then there will be times when we are called to expand that, even in a small way. As Audrey Hepburn once said, 'Take care of the small circle around you. When you have succeeded with them, then step out one small step at a time.'"—LeAnn, 54*

"It's getting even harder to place these children in America because most people are so tired of hearing about the Vietnam War," the woman added.

LeAnn couldn't live with her newfound knowledge and do nothing. "I'd like to get involved," she blurted. "Is there a number I can call to find out how I can help?"

When she walked out of that church carrying her goodies and the brochure about Friends of Children of Vietnam (FCVN), she left with much more than a dozen cupcakes—in her heart she carried the seeds of a calling from God.

LeAnn immediately began volunteering for FCVN. For the next several years, she poured her heart and energy into helping to raise money, collect supplies, and arrange adoptions for the orphans. As her volunteer responsibilities grew, so did her passion. She longed to bring one of these babies into her own life and home. After much prayer and discussion with her husband, Mark, they decided to adopt a son from Vietnam. But it was possible that Vietnam would fall before they completed the yearlong process of adoption. If Vietnam fell, no more babies would be allowed to leave.

A few weeks after filling out the adoption paperwork, LeAnn received a call from the director of FCVN. "LeAnn, would you be interested in escorting six to eight babies out of Saigon and bringing them back to their adoptive families in America? With your nursing background you're perfect for the job. But you must go knowing you probably won't be able to bring home your own son."

"I'll think and pray about it," LeAnn answered. She hung up the phone, believing this would be a great opportunity to put her skills to good use but feeling disappointed she would come home with her own arms empty.

Still, LeAnn remained faithful to her desire to help these children. She talked it over with her husband, prayed, and decided she should go. Rescuing six to eight babies seemed important enough to justify the trip.

The U.S. State Department assured LeAnn that there had been no acceleration in the war for months and that she would be safe in Saigon. However, shortly thereafter, the war intensified. Televised news showed maps of Vietnam with fierce battles raging near Saigon. The North Vietnamese dropped bombs less than three miles from the city. LeAnn watched the reports, cringing with fear and uncertainty. She wondered if she'd made the right decision.

The day before she was scheduled to leave for Saigon, LeAnn attended church as usual. When the service ended, LeAnn felt utter panic. "Honey, I need to be alone for a little bit," she said to Mark.

"Okay, we'll wait for you outside," he answered. Taking both girls by the hand, he escorted them out of the sanctuary, leaving LeAnn alone.

LeAnn sat on the pew, folded her hands in prayer, and allowed her suppressed tears to flow freely.

All the doubts and worries she had stuffed erupted from inside her like a river overflowing its banks. Her tears trickled over her folded hands as she cried out to God, "Lord, I'm terrified. Please give me a sign if I shouldn't go." Instead, she felt a clear nudge telling her the opposite. As she sat alone in the pew of the dimly lit sanctuary, a warm feeling enveloped her and her tears began to subside. Her breathing slowed to a deeper, calmer pace. Her shoulders and chest relaxed as an unexplainable feeling of courage filled her.

"Okay, Lord," she whispered. "I will go to Vietnam tomorrow."

April 1, 1975

On April Fools' Day, 1975, LeAnn and her friend Carol, also a nurse, left for Saigon.

After a grueling 24 hours of travel, LeAnn descended the airplane steps into a sweltering Saigon. The 106-degree air assaulted her, the intense heat and humidity making it difficult to breathe. Then, as she glanced around at her surroundings, reality struck. She had left a safe, free country and stepped into a dangerous war zone. Camouflage-painted aircraft and vehicles lined the runway. The unpainted airport buildings looked unfriendly. Wiping the sweat from her brow, she tried to wipe away her fear and focus on the task ahead.

As she and Carol entered the airport terminal, Cherie, an FCVN volunteer LeAnn had met in the States, raced up to them, shouting, "I'm so glad to see you two! Did you hear the news? President Ford has okayed a giant baby lift! Instead of taking out a half dozen babies, you're going to help take out nearly 300 in multiple flights . . . if we're lucky."

LeAnn, overcome with shock and joy, grinned at Carol as they soaked in the news and the importance of their remarkable mission.

On their way to the FCVN center, an animated and excited Cherie told them about a planeload of children that had barely gotten out. "The FCVN plane was waiting on the runway for permission to take off. The government hesitated to grant them permission. The plane took off anyway. One hundred and fifty children are on their way to San Francisco!" Cherie explained. "We're also scheduled to be the first evacuation flight out tomorrow. You ladies will be heading home with a plane full of children first thing in the morning."

> *"You don't have to fly to Vietnam to make a difference in the world. You can make a meal for a sick neighbor, or baby-sit someone's child. Any act of kindness improves our world."—LeAnn*

ೞ

Relief swept through LeAnn; she was anxious to return home.

As soon as she got to the orphanage, LeAnn wholeheartedly entered the desperate race to save as many of these children as possible. Operation Baby Lift was well underway. Energized by the excitement of their mission, she worked frantically all day packing the multitude of items needed to transport at least 200 babies to the United States. Carol and LeAnn spent most of the day in the two-story warehouse behind the center where the supplies were kept. They looked around at the rows of well-organized shelves and labeled boxes of supplies sent to the orphanage from the United States.

Pulling a dusty box from a rack, Carol laughed, "How do we begin to find 600 sleepers and 1,000 Pampers?"

LeAnn pulled another box from its place, staring at it. "Carol, can you believe this? This is *my* handwriting. We packed this box!"

LeAnn and Carol sorted through the familiar shirts, pants, and playsuits, delighted that these clothes would return to the U.S.—this time on an infant.

That afternoon, the Vietnamese government decided to change the schedule in retaliation against the FCVN for the plane that took off without permission. Instead, another organization would be the first allowed to leave the next day. LeAnn's heart sank at the bad news. Yet all she could do was accept the decision and continue to prepare the children.

With the change in plans, they now prepared for a transport of 100 babies to be placed onto a plane headed for Australia. Exhausted after a day of feeding, changing, cleaning, and packing for babies, LeAnn fell into bed.

The next morning LeAnn helped finalize the preparation of the babies to be transported on the plane to Australia. She sat in a VW van, with the middle seat removed, surrounded by 21 crying infants lying on the floor and the backseat. It was so hot, and because the babies were losing a lot of liquid from their tears and sweat, the volunteers worried about dehydration.

En route to the airport, they encountered a horrific traffic jam. LeAnn looked out the van window and gasped. A huge, black cloud filled the sky. She later learned from an Australian reporter that the first airplane out that morning had crashed, killing relief workers and hundreds of babies that were headed to America.

LeAnn shoved aside persistent thoughts about the implications of this tragic event. She didn't have time to think about it. Surrounding her feet, on her lap, and on both sides of her were crying, needy children. She focused on providing for them. When they got to the airport, she ignored the black cloud and helped place them on the plane. She and the other volunteers cheered as they watched the Australia-bound plane soar out of their sight toward a safe haven for the orphans.

When LeAnn returned to the center, she collapsed onto a rattan couch and sobbed uncontrollably to Cherie. "It was horrible! I can't explain the dread that overwhelmed me as I looked at that black cloud, knowing so many died in that airplane crash! I kept thinking that could happen to us." Fear-based questions filled her mind. *Will I ever see my husband and daughters again? Did God really want me to come here? Did I really hear His voice?*

"We can't think about that right now," Cherie said. "We've got lots more babies in the next room who need us right now. We need to take care of them and prepare them for evacuation."

That night at dinner, Cherie smiled at LeAnn as they ate their simple meal. She put down her fork and announced, "LeAnn, one of those babies in the next room is yours. You can be assigned one, or you can go in there and choose your son."

Stunned, LeAnn stammered, "Are you sure?"

Cherie's grin grew wider. "Yep."

LeAnn's heart raced. One of her deepest desires lay on the other side of a thin door. Earlier in the day her stomach had flipped in fear that she might die as the others had. And now, it flipped in joy. "But how can I possibly choose *one*? There are so many."

"I know it's hard. But you'll know which one is meant for your family," Cherie reassured her.

LeAnn felt she was living a fantasy—a dream come true. She hadn't allowed herself to imagine that one of these babies would be hers.

She'll never forget opening the door to the baby room. A room filled to the brim with 110 babies. The smell of spit-up, baby powder, and wet diapers filled the air, but LeAnn was oblivious to anything but the joy in her heart. The beautiful, constant hum of bawling, cooing babies sang in her ears. *How can I possibly choose* one? LeAnn asked herself again. As she stood there, a little boy wearing only a diaper crawled toward her. He crawled across the room, right into her arms and into her heart. LeAnn picked him up. Then he nestled his head into her neck. As she glanced around the room at all the babies, he kept patting her cheek with his chubby little hand and pulling her face toward him.

"Meet our son, Mitchell," LeAnn said to those gathered around. "I didn't choose him, he chose me."

For LeAnn, this moment completed the reason why God called her to Vietnam. Not only was she able to help rescue hundreds of children but she was also given the son she had longed and prayed for. It was all worth it.

But she still had to get them home.

The next day they received word that their two flights were approved for that afternoon. They rushed around packing up the first 150 children and infants for their trip to America. Cramming the children into old city buses, they slowly inched their way to the airport. When they arrived, they were informed that their flight had been delayed.

The idling bus quickly became a sauna, and the babies went ballistic. LeAnn ran up and down the aisle stroking damp foreheads and using diapers to fan red-hot faces. Eventually, they were allowed to go to some huts near the airport. There, they unloaded the babies and tried to keep them cool until the flight was ready to depart.

Mitchell was scheduled to go on the next flight with LeAnn, and thus was not on this busload of babies. The bus driver would take LeAnn back to the center to get Mitchell and the remaining children for the second flight.

As usual, nothing went as planned. Ross, another FCVN volunteer, arrived with more bad news for the workers and the babies. Holding up one finger he said, "The Vietnamese government has decided to let a plane leave, but *only one!*"

LeAnn panicked. Her heart pounded. She couldn't leave without Mitchell! She *wouldn't* leave without Mitchell.

"Get out while you can," Ross advised. "The country is closing fast. You should take my place on this plane."

"I can't," LeAnn replied, shaking with panic. "I just can't leave Mitchell—what should I do?"

Ross put his arm around her, and she buried her face in his sweat-stained shirt. Then he placed one hand on each of her shoulders and looked deeply into her eyes. "You leave now with Carol. I promise you, I will get Mitch out and bring him to you."

"But what if you don't get out? You just said that no more babies are going to be allowed to leave."

"I will. I promise you." Ross's voice cracked.

LeAnn paused and considered his idea. In her mind she felt Mark's embrace and pictured her daughters' faces. Then she imagined what might happen to Mitchell if he ended up in the hands of the Vietcong.

"I can't leave Mitchell here to be tortured or killed. I won't leave without him," she resolved.

LeAnn jumped on the bus and, through an interpreter, asked the driver to take her back to the center. Her plan was to race back to the center, grab Mitchell, and race back to the airport before the plane took off.

The bus driver sped recklessly back to the center. The crowded streets, the hundreds of weaving bicycles, the endless stream of cars, all angered LeAnn as the bus honked and jerked through the snarling traffic.

"Come on, can't you go any faster?" she hollered at the driver who didn't speak a word of English.

He stopped the bus about a mile from the center. He opened the door, smiled at LeAnn, and pointed down a narrow street ahead. She jumped off the bus and sprinted as fast as her legs would carry her. The strap of her sandal broke and her shoe smacked against her ankle. She reached down without stopping, grabbed her sandal, yanked it off, and ran with one bare foot. When she made it to the center she was practically hyperventilating. "Where's Mitchell?" she gasped. "I need Mitchell, NOW!"

"LeAnn, calm down," Cherie said, meeting her at the door. "I just spoke with an airport official. He called to say the plane would wait for you." She smiled. "And he told me the second flight has been re-approved."

"Thank You, God," was all LeAnn could manage to say.

From that moment on, LeAnn didn't let Mitchell out of her sight. He and the other babies were placed in cardboard boxes, two to three babies per box, and loaded onto the cargo planes. The planes landed safely 24 hours later on American soil, filled with 300 babies, one being LeAnn's newest family member.

Never in her wildest dreams did LeAnn imagine that she would take part in a huge effort to evacuate children. She simply followed God's tug on her heart to buy a few cupcakes—and then followed His leading, step by step, through her heart's desire, to make a difference in the lives of unwanted children. Through her obedience, God incrementally increased her responsibilities and put her in a position to be used to help others. "When I went to Vietnam, I had no idea what was going to happen. I just followed this nudging in my heart and then received blessing beyond my imagination."

> *"The calling I felt was a nudging that wouldn't go away. It was a deep inner voice that kept pestering me."—LeAnn*

In Their Footsteps

"I've let God guide me to places of service and I've found joy comes from serving. Always think about others and try to encourage them."
—*Pat, 72*

"Take time on a regular basis to nourish your heart and soul. This needs to involve some time of quiet listening so you can hear that still, small voice. Nothing is more important than listening and responding to God."
—*Donna, 55*

"Never take life for granted. Live each day to the fullest. God put each of us here for a purpose, and we need to live that purpose out to the fullest."
—*Jane, 59*

"My advice to women is to do things for others; don't just do things for yourself. The more you do, the more you're going to get back."
—*Elizabeth, 95*

Wanda

Wanda, who went from housewife to lobbyist,
fixed a big problem and found peace for
her troubled soul along the way.

Wanda was angry at God and the world. Sitting alone at her kitchen table, she glimpsed a headline in the local paper that caused her blood to boil. She jabbed at the paper with her finger. "God, why would You allow someone like this guy to live but take my Jeremy away?"

Her tears flowed and disappeared into her coffee cup. It just didn't make any sense. She closed her eyes, and thoughts of her son filled her mind. *Jeremy was the model child. He had such a sweet spirit; he loved his family and friends. I know he made a big mistake; he used poor judgement, but he didn't deserve to die!* "I'm going crazy," Wanda said aloud to no one. "I need help or I'm going to go nuts."

The past year had been a blur. Jeremy and his friend had driven from Texas across the border into Louisiana to party. Everyone near the border knew you just had to be tall enough to reach the bar and you could get alcohol in Louisiana. On their way home, the driver of the car, whose blood alcohol level was above the legal limit, crashed—abruptly ending Jeremy's life. And now, Wanda felt like ending her own life.

God, I can't go on like this. I know my husband, my kids, and my grandkids all need me. I'm no good to anyone in this state of mind. She grabbed the phone book and looked up the toll-free phone number for MADD—Mothers Against Drunk Driving—something she now cared about. Maybe they could help her.

> *"When you're angry at God, tell Him what's on your mind. Talk to Him. He'll listen."—Wanda, 59*

The person on the other end of the receiver directed her to her local chapter. She called them and simply said, "I need some kind of help; can you send me some brochures or something?"

A few days later she received a big, fat packet in the mail.

She opened it and quickly perused the volume of information. Suddenly, one sentence stopped her cold. It said, "Now that the drinking age of 21 has been established in all 50 states. . . ."

"Well, that's a lie!" she screamed at the deaf packet of information. Furious that such a respected organization would send out such an untruth made her head spin with anger. She promptly called her local MADD chapter and gave them a piece of her mind.

"How can you publish such an untruth! I can't believe you would print that the law says the drinking age of 21 has been established in all 50 states. Everyone in Texas knows that's not the case for Louisiana."

"Ma'am," a very patient man said, "a lot of folks in Louisiana are angry too. There's an ongoing group that has been trying to change Louisiana's drinking law for years. I'll give you their phone number."

She didn't get the answer that she wanted from him, so she began her own investigation. After numerous phone calls, she decided she needed to read the law for herself. Finally, she received a copy of it. The law forbade the purchase, possession, and consumption of alcohol by anyone under 21, but it didn't prohibit the sale.

She stared at the law, stunned. The wording was ridiculous, but someone, somewhere had eventually realized that the ambiguous wording left the responsibility on the shoulders of the minor instead of the seller. The vendor could sell all the liquor he wanted to whomever he wanted without the penalty of law. Only the minor could be charged—if he was caught.

That's absurd! I can't believe it! How many kids have died because of that loophole? She fumed as understanding of the law became clear to her.

The more Wanda researched this law, the angrier she became. Wanda made a vow. *Jeremy's death will not be in vain. I'll do all I can to get that law changed.*

First, Wanda wrote a letter to the local PTA. She made copies to hand out to everyone she knew. After this, people began inviting her to speak at different educational and civic organizations. Within three months, she was speaking before the governor and attorney general for the state of Louisiana. She was telling her story and starting the fight to change the law—to add the phrase that it is illegal to sell alcohol to anyone under the age of 21.

Wanda quickly went from housewife to lobbyist. One day, she received a call from the sheriff's department. "Wanda, don't forget about the press conference tomorrow. We hope you can make it," the young woman said.

Press conference? What in the world is a press conference? Wanda wondered to herself. "Oh, don't y'all worry," she said aloud, unwilling to reveal her ignorance. "I'll definitely be there."

The press conference was held at the Welcome Center just inside the Texas border. The purpose was to raise public awareness about the problem Texas faced as young people drove across the border and, within just two miles, found bars that legally served alcohol to minors. Then they recklessly drove back home. After a few speakers, the young woman who had called Wanda leaned over and said, "You're next. Are you ready?"

"What?" Wanda asked.

"Go talk," she said.

Wanda's palms began sweating, and her mouth dried up. *I don't know what I'm going to say, Lord. Give me the words.*

Wanda bravely stood up before the crowd and began, "I didn't want to be a fanatic, I just wanted to be Jeremy's mother." Then she told the tragic story of how Jeremy died. She shared her thoughts and opinions about the ridiculous law that led to the death of her son. She continued, "During my research, I discovered that on a 30-mile stretch of highway running from Texas to Louisiana—the stretch of highway where Jeremy and his friend died—64 children have been killed in drunk-driving incidents within one year. If this law is not changed, it will only lead to the deaths of hundreds more. This is an ignorant law for profit. These deaths will not end until we decide to value lives over profit." She ended as the crowd erupted in loud applause.

That night, she appeared on the local television news and the next morning, her picture was on the front page of the local paper. From there, she appeared on the front page of *The New York Times* and was featured on several local and national television news programs.

Thanks to her efforts and the attention it brought to a serious problem, Louisiana changed its law. Four years after Jeremy's death, the Louisiana Supreme Court closed the liquor loophole. It became illegal for bars to sell alcohol to anyone under 21. Once again, as Wanda sat at her kitchen table, her phone rang. It was a secretary from the Louisiana State Supreme Court Services calling to tell her the good news.

"You got it, Wanda. You got it!"

Wanda hung up the phone and cried. "Thank You, God." Then, looking up toward the ceiling, she said, "Look, Jeremy darlin'. You and the other boys—look what we've done."

Although Louisiana's law was changed, the ambiguously written federal law is still in place. Wanda's battle continues as she tries to have the federal law rewritten to close the possibility of further loopholes.

"I still have a lot of questions for God," Wanda says. "When I get to heaven I'm going to have a long appointment with Him. But I have found some peace, knowing that Jeremy's death resulted in changing this law that will save hundreds of other kids, lives. Who can say? One of those kids, a kid I will never know and who will never know me, might even become president someday."

In Their Footsteps

"God can take all the anger you may be feeling, so it is okay to be mad at Him. He gave you all your emotions, so He is fully aware of all of them. Give Him your hurt, worry, sorrow, guilt, fear, and anxiety. He will replace them with His peace, His love, and His joy."
—*Linette, 50*

"This too shall pass. Trials and suffering build character and although we would never choose to go through them, we almost always come out stronger and a little more resilient. Don't let them break you; try to believe that God knew all about them, is in the midst of them, and will use them to the glory of His kingdom, if we allow Him to."
—*Anonymous, 62*

"It is impossible to overcome suffering without a faith that is firmly planted. God will see you through any situation if you trust Him."
—*Connie, whose daughter was killed*
by a drunk driver

"I've learned you shouldn't go through life with a catcher's mitt on both hands. You need to be able to throw something back."
—*Anonymous, 64*

June

*Through more than 21 years of ministering to
teens, June delightfully discovered that the more
lives she touched, the more blessed she became.*

Just as June put the last dinner dish into the dishwasher, her phone
rang.

"Hi, June, this is Leslie," said her friend from church.

"Oh, hi there. Hey, how's it going with your niece?" June asked as
she balanced the receiver between her jaw and shoulder and grabbed a
dishtowel to wipe the countertop around her sink. "I heard she moved
in last week. What is her name?"

"Jessie, and frankly, she's the reason I'm calling you."

"Why? What's going on?"

"Well, as you know, her mom died when she and her triplet sisters
were not yet a year old. Then her dad married several different wives,
none that Jessie and her sisters liked. And none that really seemed to love
them. Now, with three wild teenage girls, her dad is having such a hard
time. He decided to split them up. When I said Jessie could live with us,
I really didn't know what I was getting myself into. I think she needs to
be around some kids her own age. Kids who will be a good influence on

her," Leslie explained. "Since you're the sponsor for the Bible Bowl at church, I was wondering if she could go with you tonight."

"Sure, Luke and I would love to come pick her up. We'll be at your house around 6:30," June said and hung up the phone.

"Who was that, Mom?" Luke, her 16-year-old son asked as he reached into the fridge to pour himself another glass of milk to dip his cookie into. Her husband, Ed, also curious about the phone call, peeked his head around the kitchen corner to hear her answer.

> *"I recognize that many people from various generations helped and shaped me. I know the merging of generations has been a way that God has used me in teenagers' lives."—June, 58*

"You know Leslie from church? Her niece Jessie moved in with them for a while. I guess she's lived with lots of different families and now she's living with Leslie. She asked if we would take her to Bible Bowl tonight."

⁓

"And, of course, you said yes. Right?" Luke said as he dunked his last bite of cookie into the milk.

"That's great," Ed added. "I wonder if she's ever been to a Bible study before."

"I have no idea. But come on, Luke," she said, snapping him with the kitchen towel to hurry him up. "Go get ready. We need to leave a little early."

June and Luke drove up to Leslie's house, honked the horn, and waited for Jessie to appear. As Jessie walked out the front door, Luke said, "Wow, she's tall! How tall do you think she is? Over six feet I bet."

"Luke, be nice. Let's make her feel welcome."

As Jessie walked to the car, June noticed her tomboy-like gait and her drab outfit of baggy, faded blue jeans and an untucked T-shirt. Unlike most girls her age, she didn't have on lots of makeup. *She looks like a girl who's never had a mom. Poor thing, I can only imagine how hard her life has been.*

Jessie opened the door and plopped herself down in the backseat of the car.

Luke and June looked over their shoulders to greet her.

"Hi, Jessie. I'm June and this is my son Luke. You two are about the same age."

"Hey," Jessie responded. "So where are we going? Some Bible thing, my aunt said." Jessie twisted her long, straight hair around her finger and stared out the window.

"Yep, it's called Bible Bowl," June answered.

"Bible Bowl? What kind of name is that? It sounds like something you eat."

"No, it's kind of like a Bible study, only it's a game," June explained. "We study the Bible together then ask questions about the passages we've studied. You're on a team and you compete against other teams. A judge will ask a question,

> *"Jesus knew the importance of adults in the lives of children, even those not of our immediate family. Mark tells us, 'He took the children in His arms, put His hands on them and blessed them.' If Jesus realized the importance of loving, touching, and blessing children, so should I."—June*

and the first group to hit the buzzer gets a chance to answer the question. It's a competition. You win points when you get the answer right."

"Oh, is it like *bowling* for dollars? Do you win any money?" Jessie asked.

"No, but sometimes you can win trophies, or scholarships to good Christian colleges."

"Sounds *really* fun," Jessie said, her voice dripping with sarcasm.

"It is really fun," June answered. "This semester we're studying the letters in the New Testament written by John."

"New Testament? What's that?"

Oh boy! She absolutely, positively knows nothing about the Bible. She's going to be a real challenge. But hey, I like challenges.

"Umm . . . I'll explain that to you later. First, tell us a little about yourself," June replied as she sneaked a sideways peek at her son Luke with a look that said, *Say something pleeeeze!*

"Yeah," Luke said, "like, why are you living with your aunt?" June rolled her eyes at Luke's blunt personal question. *That's not what I had in mind. But Luke never was one to beat around the bush.*

"I guess my two sisters and I were just too much trouble for step-mom number three. She couldn't handle us. But then again, we did make it our job to make her miserable," Jessie smirked.

"Why? What did you do to her?" Luke asked.

"Well, lots of stuff. I guess what really made her mad was this time when we took her car engine apart. She really liked to drive and shop and stuff like that. Our dad taught us a lot about mechanics, so one day we went in and messed up the engine on her car."

"Cool!"

"Luke, don't get any ideas now," June chimed in.

"Well, it cost like $700 to fix it. That's when our dad told us we had to go live with our aunts and uncles. So now I guess I'm here for two years. Then when I graduate from high school, I'm outta here."

Week after week, June and Luke picked up Jessie. She went from poking fun at the Bible study to becoming curious. As her competitive spirit kicked in, she began to enjoy the competitions. She faithfully attended church and seemed to enjoy the kids she was making friends with. After a couple of months, a real miracle happened.

One Sunday the pastor of the church gave an invitation for anyone who wanted to give their life to Christ to come forward. June saw Jessie's familiar gait and her head towering over the others as she walked up to the front of the church and knelt at the altar. June quickly wiped the tears from her eyes. She knew Jessie wouldn't like to see her cry. But the joy June experienced at that moment made it impossible for her not to let a few tears fall.

About six weeks later, June received a call from Jessie. Through her sobs she explained that her dad had died in a car accident. Now, Jessie didn't have a mother or a father, and her sisters recently rejected her because of her newfound faith.

Her aunt, Leslie, was doing the best she could, but Jessie and June shared a special relationship. Recognizing their unique bond, Leslie didn't mind as June took on the primary role as Jessie's guardian. June attended Jessie's parent-teacher conferences. Jessie often joined their family on vacations. June went out to eat with Jessie and they would talk and pray together.

When they traveled to Bible Bowl competitions, June and Jessie often shared a hotel room. At these getaways Jessie loved to talk to June late into the night. Oftentimes, she talked about her sisters. She missed them terribly and was hurt by their rejection. She asked tough questions about God and why He would take her mother and father. She said whatever was on her mind. Just as June would drift off into sleep she'd hear, "Hey, June." Jessie would talk some more and June would listen. Occasionally, June would offer advice. Mostly, it seemed Jessie just wanted someone to listen.

During Jessie's senior year, the team she was on won a national competition and she was awarded a full scholarship to a college in Missouri. *Well, her roommate will sure get an education,* June thought as she reflected on Jessie's rough-around-the-edges personality. *But she's sure changed and grown remarkably in the last two years. I think she's going to make it!* June smiled and waved good-bye to Jessie as she boarded a bus and ventured off to college.

And make it she did. Four years later, Jessie graduated from college and is now a missionary in Colombia. One of her projects is gathering Christian books in Spanish to put in libraries around that country.

Jessie is just one of a hundred examples of teenagers impacted by June during her 21 years of ministering to teens at her church. The teenagers became her extended family. She had them in her home, traveled thousands of miles with them, shared in their victories and disappointments, and discussed how to deal with many of life's situations.

She believes her children benefited from her involvement in this ministry. "Knowing and loving someone like Jessie taught my kids tolerance for people who are different. They loved being around the teenagers when they were little, and the teens loved my kids. As my own children became teenagers, they were a part of this group. Yet my children never doubted I was their mom and loved them. As adults, they are eager to help other people and are sensitive to their needs. I think this stems back to the time we spent helping teens."

> *"As a mom, nothing has been more important to me than my children knowing and serving the Lord. It's much more important than sports, school activities, jobs, or any of the hundreds of demands on their lives."—June*

⟨◌⟩

Ed, her husband, often drove the church bus and also became involved in these kids' lives. One time, Jessie told June that her marriage to Ed was the first model of a good marriage she had ever seen.

Today, June feels a little part of her, through "her kids," has touched lives all over the world. "Many of my kids are now serving the Lord all over the U.S., China, Colombia, Kenya, Taiwan, India, Kosovo, Mexico, and Chile." They serve in all different areas of the church as pastors, Sunday school teachers, music and Bible study sponsors, and even Bible Bowl sponsors.

"I was often asked if I got discouraged, and my answer was always 'Are you kidding? Of course!' I'd get so upset and I often wondered why I invested my life in these kids. Now, I see many answers, and it is well worth every tear, every headache, and a full head of gray hair."

In Their Footsteps

"If it takes a village to raise a child, then it takes a family of God to make a child understand how personal and mighty our God really is. My children had the privilege of belonging to a group of people who talked about God as easily as they talked about brushing their teeth."
        —*Anonymous*

"We served the Lord together as a family. We were a singing family and loved to sing songs of worship together. Our children were our helpers as they participated in our visits to convalescent homes or sang together on radio and television programs."
        —*Roxie, 85. She feels that her family's ministering to*
            others through singing had a powerful impact on
            her five children's spiritual growth.

"The best way to teach your children is through your own actions. As a family, we used to volunteer to serve Thanksgiving dinner to the homeless. It was always such a great experience. Now, my three adult children do this with their own kids each year."
        —*Jessie, 74*

"I spend a lot of time doing work for the church, working with youth, and volunteering at our local hospital. Everyone says, 'You're working too hard; you're going to burn out.' But I know I won't because I am doing what the Lord wants me to do."
        —*Hazel, 76*

Dora

*When breast cancer threatened to claim
Dora's life, she leaned on her friends and they
carried her through her crisis.*

Dora walked into her favorite restaurant and scanned the room, look-ing for her two good friends, DeeDee and Gretchen. *There they are. Oh, Lord, how am I going to tell them the bad news?* she thought as she walked over to their table. When she gave them each a friendly squeeze, Dora could feel the sharp, stinging pain on the side of her right breast where the doctor had just taken a biopsy of a peanut-shaped lump she had discovered during her monthly self-exam.

"Well," DeeDee asked, "what did the doctor say?"

"It doesn't look good. I won't know anything for sure until tomor-row, but he thinks it's probably cancer."

"Oh, Dora, I'm so sorry," Gretchen said as tears began to form in her eyes. "What are you going to do?" The three of them sat in silence for a few minutes. Her friends were at a loss for words; nothing seemed appropriate. Besides, it wasn't for sure—yet.

"I'll be fine. Don't even worry about it. Right now, let's just enjoy lunch," Dora said as she sipped her cold water and tried to push her fears to the back of her mind.

The next day the doctor called and confirmed what Dora feared. She had breast cancer. After calling her husband, Bruce, she called DeeDee, who coordinated the prayer chain at church. Then Dora broke the bad news to her 17-year-old daughter.

"Well, Christina, we have bad news. It's definitely cancer." Dora tried not to cry as she explained the diagnosis to her daughter, but she couldn't hold back the tears. The sobbing came. The reality of what this meant to her family caused the floodgates to burst open.

"Mom, does this mean that I am probably going to get cancer too?" Christina voiced the question every daughter whose mother has had breast cancer wants answered.

> *"When I was 33, the doctors removed a benign tumor. After that, I started getting annual mammograms and doing self-exams each month after each period. I recommend women do these self-exams; it can save lives."—Dora, 49*

"Oh, honey," Dora said, wrapping her arms around her daughter. "Because I have cancer, you are at a higher risk of also having it. But with good healthy living and a lot of close watching, you should be okay. But let's not worry about it right now, you're so young. I'll do whatever I can to fight this battle and to trust the Lord with my life. You have to do the same."

Although the rug had been pulled out from under Dora's feet, she didn't want it to be pulled out from under her daughter and husband. As she read about breast cancer, she realized she had a chronic disease. Most likely, breast cancer would be her battle for months, if not years. Dora desired to keep her husband's and daughter's life as normal as possible. She didn't want to add to their stress and worry about her. She desperately wanted to try and be the wife and mother they needed—to love and serve them, not to burden them. To do that, she knew she needed the help of her friends. She allowed herself to humbly accept their service.

Dora's first step was to choose from a long list of treatment options. After talking through the different options with her husband and friends, she prayed. *Lord, I'm only 45 years old. I want the next 45 years to be even better than the first. I need help with this choice; give me wisdom on what I should do.* The most drastic option involved an immediate single mastectomy and reconstructive surgery followed by the highest doses of chemotherapy a human body allows. She chose this option. As she met with the plastic surgeon to discuss the surgery, he mentioned that due to her size, he would not be able to match the breasts. "I would recommend a reduction of your other breast to match the one we're reconstructing," he explained.

"If you're going to go in and take tissue out, you might as well do a double mastectomy and reconstruction of both my breasts," Dora reasoned. "It seems ridiculous to do a reduction if my chances of getting cancer in my other breast are high anyway. I would rather just get rid of it, and increase my chances for survival."

Dora had declared war on her cancer. She now looked at her breasts as her enemy. They were trying to kill her and she wanted to live.

Bruce and most of her friends supported her in this decision. However, a few friends questioned her logic, thinking she was too radical. "Dora, are you sure you're doing the wisest thing?" asked one friend as they walked on a paved path next to a creek. "Do you think it's really necessary to go through a double mastectomy and reconstruction? It seems so drastic."

"You know," Dora answered, "I've prayed about this so much and I've come to realize my sexuality is not tied to my breasts. I don't need them anymore. They served their purpose. They fed my babies. And Bruce is fine with this. My breasts are now a threat to my life. After everything I've read, I believe my best chance to beat this cancer is my first chance. It's now."

When Dora returned home from the radical surgery, she was

bedridden for nearly three months. The surgeons had first removed all breast tissue. Then they cut into her abdominal muscles, pulling them up to her chest to create new breasts. This extreme procedure caused excruciating pain in her torso. She could barely roll out of bed. During Dora's recovery, Gretchen and DeeDee coordinated prayers, meals, house cleaners, visitors, and even people to sit with Bruce during her surgeries. They took care of just about everything. And their loving care allowed Bruce to return to work with the assurance that Dora was in good hands.

As time went on, they paid close attention to Dora's needs and devised creative ways to help her.

Because the pain made it impossible for Dora to turn her head from side to side or to look over her shoulder, she couldn't drive. So her friends coordinated drivers to take Dora to her doctor's appointments.

Moving from day to day through the debilitating pain was hard enough. But the physical pain wasn't nearly as difficult as the emotional pain. One of her lowest times came when she and Gretchen went shopping for wigs, as Dora antici-

> *"My friends knew how hard it was for me to be inactive, so they scheduled a few trips to take me up to the mountains for a night or two. This change of scenery meant the world to me."—Dora*

pated the day when her hair would fall out from the intense doses of chemotherapy. They first visited the local American Cancer Society office, where people donate wigs when they don't need them anymore.

"Here's a nice one," Gretchen said as she held up a light brown wig. "It's just about the same color as your hair. And the cut is pretty cute."

"Yeah, that one's okay," Dora said, feeling gloomier than ever. She put the wig on and looked at herself in the mirror, unable to control her dark thoughts. *I wonder if the woman who wore this one is still alive?* Tears filled her eyes. *What if I'm not living a year from now?*

Gretchen put an arm around Dora's shoulder. "Dora, I know this must be hard and very scary for you. It's okay to cry." After a hug and some more tears, Gretchen handed her a tissue and went to search out the perfect wig for her sad, scared friend.

It didn't take long before her hair started to fall out. Dora didn't want this process to drag on. She didn't want to find little tufts of hair on her pillow, or on her couch and clothes. So she called Susan, a friend with four boys, and asked her to bring over the clippers she used to cut her boys' hair. Dora wanted her head shaved.

"Dora, are you ready?" Susan asked, with clippers buzzing in her hand, the sound sending a shiver down Dora's spine and a weakness to her knees.

"Yep, I'm ready. I know I can't control this cancer, but I want to control when and where my hair will fall out," Dora bravely answered. "I never thought I would be the first one to go bald in my marriage," she joked, trying to make light of a horrible moment.

Susan began buzzing off Dora's hair. The pile of locks grew around her feet and fell onto the towel she had carefully wrapped around her shoulders. Dora's heart flip-flopped when suddenly, they heard the front door open and the sound of young girls' voices.

"Oh no!" Dora said to Susan, clutching the towel to her chest. "Christina and her friends are here. She'll be so uncomfortable—especially with her friends." Dora looked up at Susan, feeling fear and great sadness in the core of her being. "I didn't want her to see me like this."

"That's okay," Susan said. "We'll clean up."

But it was too late. The girls walked into the kitchen searching for an after-school snack. Their eyes widened and their mouths dropped as they took in Dora, who sat wrapped in a towel on a kitchen stool with half of her head shaved. Hair covered the floor around her. Susan stood upright, holding the clippers that had done their damage. No one knew what to say.

"Mom! What are you doing? Why are you having your hair shaved off?" Christina asked.

"Oh, honey, you know how I told you my hair would probably fall out. Well, it started and I didn't want to find my own hair all over the house, so I asked Susan to shave it off. I'm sorry, I didn't know you were coming home right now."

The teenage girls made a quick exit, obviously uncomfortable at seeing Dora in this condition.

"Dora," Susan said, "you handled that really well. She'll be okay." Susan tried to say words to encourage Dora while she finished the job. But as Dora looked into the hand mirror at her fuzzy head, she felt ashamed and embarrassed. *Boy, my head is really ugly. I look mean. I look like a convict who just escaped from prison.* She rubbed her fingers over the newly discovered ridges that sat behind her ears. *These look really ugly; I never knew I had bumps here.*

"Well, dear, we're done," Susan said as she cleaned up the floor. Dora put on one of her wigs and helplessly smiled at her friend. "You look smashing!" Susan gave Dora a hug as she left.

This wouldn't be the first time in her journey of recovery that Dora would feel humbled. Helpless to even clean her own house because of her pain, friends would clean for her—even scrub the dirty toilets and bathroom floors. One woman and her sons came every other week for six months to clean. While she and her 11-year-old scrubbed Dora's four bathrooms, the five-year-old wandered around the house with a feather duster, dusting all the baseboards.

One time Dora was pleasantly surprised at the house cleaners who appeared on her doorstep. After hearing the doorbell ring, she slowly inched her away to the door and opened it to see a couple of goofy-looking women, wearing shabby, obnoxiously mismatched clothes, brightly colored wigs, and big straw hats with gaudy flowers protruding like alien antennae from the tops of their heads. All Dora could do was laugh—and even that hurt.

"Hi, we're here to clean your house," they stated. Although it was hard to understand them through their fake noses and ugly false teeth, Dora recognized the voice of one of them, a friend from church.

"You go on and lie down. We know your husband and daughter are at Bible study tonight so we came to clean while they're gone." Dora, still laughing, stepped aside and waved them in. She couldn't refuse their offer; they were enjoying themselves and boy did they ever clean!

During this time, Dora's relationship with God deepened. She had lots of time to pray and read the Bible. She felt His presence, and she accepted and appreciated little gifts He would send her way—things she used to consider annoying. Like the neighbor kitty who would perch outside her bedroom window and keep her company. Or the deer that wandered into her yard and chewed on her bushes.

She also learned to be content and not take life for granted.

After six surgeries and six months of chemotherapy, the doctors have declared Dora cancer-free. There's always a risk of the cancer returning, but Dora doesn't dwell on that.

Today, she volunteers for a cancer support group. "I decided I wanted to give back and help others struggling through cancer." She coordinates activities for these women—like weekly walks and exercise sessions. In the winter she plans monthly snowshoe hikes. She offers an understanding, listening ear. "It's a hard ministry. I know some of the women I'm building friendships with are going to die. Today, my friends who helped me through my cancer still help by praying for this ministry."

Dora can't even find words to express her thankfulness to her friends and their support of her and her family during her fight with cancer. However, through their example of love, devotion, and service, she knows more about being a friend in the good times and the bad. "Cultivate friendships and spiritual life when you're well. Because when the messes come, you will need your faith, family, and especially your friends to carry you through."

In Their Footsteps

"Pray without ceasing. Share your troubles with others who will pray for you."

—Dawn, 55, a breast cancer survivor

"Don't try to keep up a good front; use your friends and their comfort."

—Anonymous 61-year-old survivor
of cancer and divorce

"To any young woman experiencing a tragedy or illness, I would say, first you have to accept it, embrace the fact you have it, and remember God has a purpose even in this."

—Ruby, 69

"When I had breast cancer, I tried not to say 'I have cancer.' Instead I would say, 'I'm on the Jesus journey to conquer cancer.' I think having a positive mind-set helps."

—Hazel, 76

Compassion Summary

⌒

Compassion = Love in Action

Any act of kindness toward someone else can change a life. Most women are compassion addicts. Women love to help others. Because of this attitude, women make the world a better place.

Not only do these acts of kindness benefit the receivers but the givers are blessed as well. LeAnn, Wanda, June, and Dora's friends selflessly put their love into action and reaped incredible rewards. You don't have to fly to Vietnam like LeAnn, or become a lobbyist like Wanda (although you could if you wanted to)—but any of us can do what June's or Dora's friends did. We can all build meaningful relationships with those around us and impact someone's life forever.

Whatever good deed you think you might want to do, go beyond thinking about it—go and do it!

What women do you admire who made a difference in your life? What did they do to help you?

Have you had any thoughts or nudgings that you think might be from God? What are they?

Why do you think God made women so compassionate?

Think of a woman who puts her love into action. What does she do? What traits does she possess that you admire?

Suggestions:

1. Think of one kind deed you can do to help someone today and do it (e.g., make cookies for a neighbor, take your child and a friend out for lunch, visit an elderly woman).

2. If you've experienced a hardship in some area—like the death of a child or some form of abuse—join a group to help others with that same issue (e.g., become a victim's advocate or lead a small grief group).

3. Look for a need in your community and do something to help meet that need (e.g., organize a food drive at your child's school for a homeless shelter in your community or collect teddy bears and donate to the police department for kids in crisis).

Walk On!

We hope the stories and quotes in this book have shown you that you can draw on the wisdom and life experiences of older women not only to survive but to triumph over whatever life throws at you. We also hope these stories help you to see that women who have walked before you know a lot about marriage, about parenting, about singleness, about God—about life!

For the past several years, as we've met, surveyed, and interviewed hundreds of women, we've walked away with a couple of important truths and we want to pass them on to you as you seek an older friend to guide you.

We noticed that the women we interviewed who were the most positive, joy-filled, inspirational, and encouraging women all had something in common: At some point in their life, they had made a couple of critical choices. First, they chose to follow Christ and live according to His example. Then, they made an attitude choice. They chose to use whatever circumstance they found themselves in for good—for themselves and for the benefit of others. They chose to be blessed not bitter. They chose not to remain victims but to move beyond victim to victor. They chose to *live* victoriously. They chose to trust God more than themselves—more than anything or anyone else. They chose to engage in relationships with others rather than live a secluded, lonely life. They chose to see the good in every situation rather than wallow in the negative. They chose to forgive rather than harbor feelings of bitterness toward someone who had hurt them. These choices resulted in peace, joy, and blessings beyond what they would have imagined. So we encourage you to look for a dedicated Christian woman who approaches life with a very positive attitude.

Also, after writing this book, we're *positively, absolutely* convinced that nothing can replace the value of an older, wiser woman walking alongside you in life—teaching, training, and encouraging you to be the woman God wants you to be. Many good resources exist to help us in this journey of life, but nothing can take the place of a living, breathing, feeling woman who's experienced life firsthand.

Life is a journey—a walk. It is delightful. It is unpredictable. Sometimes life is like an easy stroll through a peaceful park. Other times it's a steep hill that leaves you breathless and exhausted. Every once in a while, you take a wrong turn and feel completely and utterly lost and confused. Sometimes life is moving so fast that you feel like you're sprinting into each new day. At times, life is exhilarating and awe-inspiring. Other times it's so painful that all you can do is fall on your knees and crawl, inch by inch, forward.

No matter what circumstances cross your path in life, you don't have to walk through them alone. You can find an older woman to guide you on this journey—a woman walking ahead of you. She can warn you about the steep, rocky hills and encourage you that the view at the top is worth the climb. She'll help you choose which streets to explore when you're at a crossroads because she's faced similar decisions in her lifetime. She knows those dark alleys to avoid. She knows that sometimes the walk is long and hard but because she's been there before you, she knows what you will need. She'll point out the breathtaking views and make sure you're not walking with your head down, missing all the incredible sights along this walk through life. She'll help you discover and become the woman you were designed to be.

We can't think of anything better than to encourage you to seek out an older, wiser woman and ask her to be your guide on this crazy life journey. Pray that God will lead you to a woman you can befriend. Don't be afraid to approach an older woman and ask her if she would meet with you. As you ask her questions like "What do you know now that you wish you had known when you were my age?" you'll be amazed at the wisdom she has to offer. If you don't have a woman in mind, then ask your pastor to hook you up with someone. Or attend a women's Bible study and look for a woman to mentor you. Whatever it takes, do it.

As you close this book, we hope these stories and the wisdom from these women will stay in your heart and encourage you on your journey. But mostly, we hope you will go out and seek a mentor—build a friendship with an older woman. Walk through life together, and experience the joy and strength that comes from this unique friendship.

Encouragement for Women
at Every Stage of Life
From Focus on the Family®!

• • •

Dreams of a Woman

Girlhood dreams shape almost every woman's life. But what happens when those dreams seem to be on hold—or denied? In *Dreams of a Woman*, author Sharon Jaynes encourages women to reconsider their desires and allow God to surpass their dreams. Includes Bible study questions.

Who Holds the Key to Your Heart

God offers love, hope, forgiveness and healing. Lysa TerKeurst, who has dealt with her own secret shame, will help you identify your pain and lead you to hope and healing through Scripture, testimonials, study questions and more. Come break the bondage deep within and be set free!

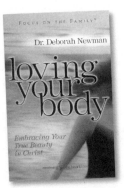

Loving Your Body

Do you think you must look just right to be accepted and loved? Do you agonize about cellulite, crow's feet, jello thighs and bad hair weeks? In *Loving Your Body*, beauty myths are swept away by a powerful revelation of God's heart toward you.

Apples of Gold

Discover a program that takes seriously the biblical admonition for older women to mentor younger women. Learn about how to set up an "Apples of Gold" study group including what personnel and funding are needed and scheduling and planning. Lessons on kindness, loving your husband and children, submission, purity and hospitality are based on Titus 2:3-5.

• • •

Look for these special books in your Christian bookstore. To request a copy, call (800) A-FAMILY (232-6459), log on to www.family.org/resources or write to Focus on the Family, Colorado Springs, CO 80995.

Visit our Web site (www.family.org) to learn more about the ministry or find out if there is a Focus on the Family office in your country.